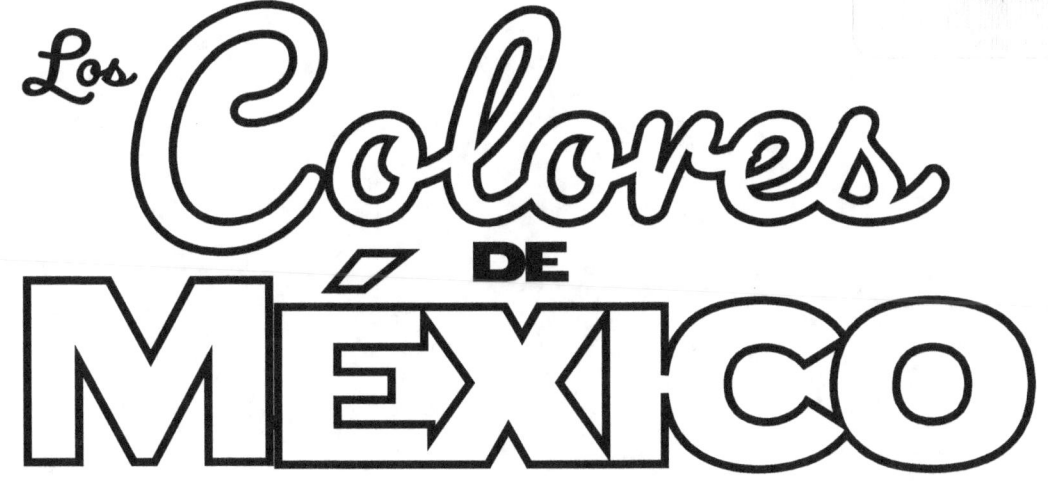

This book belongs to...
Este libro es de...

_____

Published in 2020 by Juventud Enriquecimiento Musica y Artes Foundation
© Juventud Enriquecimiento Musica y Artes (JEMA) Foundation 2020
All Rights Reserved
www.jemafoundation.org

ISBN: 9798582144038

No part of this book may be reproduced or transmitted in whole or in part, in any form or by any means, electronic or mechanical, including photocopying, digitized, recording or by any information storage, and retrieval system, without the written permission from the publisher.

Please do not distribute any uncolored pages in any form including posting on social media, uploading to any website, or through any other method. You may post colored pages on social media sites, but not limited to, Facebook, Twitter, Instagram, and Pinterest. You may scan and print the images for personal use so you can color them multiple times or print them on a different sheet of paper. Please do not sell any colored images from this book for profit. All images remain copyright of JEMA Foundation.

Los Colores de Mexico is an imprint owned by JEMA Foundation.
Los Colores de Mexico brand coloring pages are created by a team of independent artists.

Printed in the U.S.A.

JEMA Foundation
Post Office Box 845
Visalia, California 93292

Have questions or concerns? Let us know.
jemafoundation.org | info@jemafoundation.org

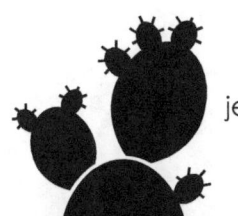

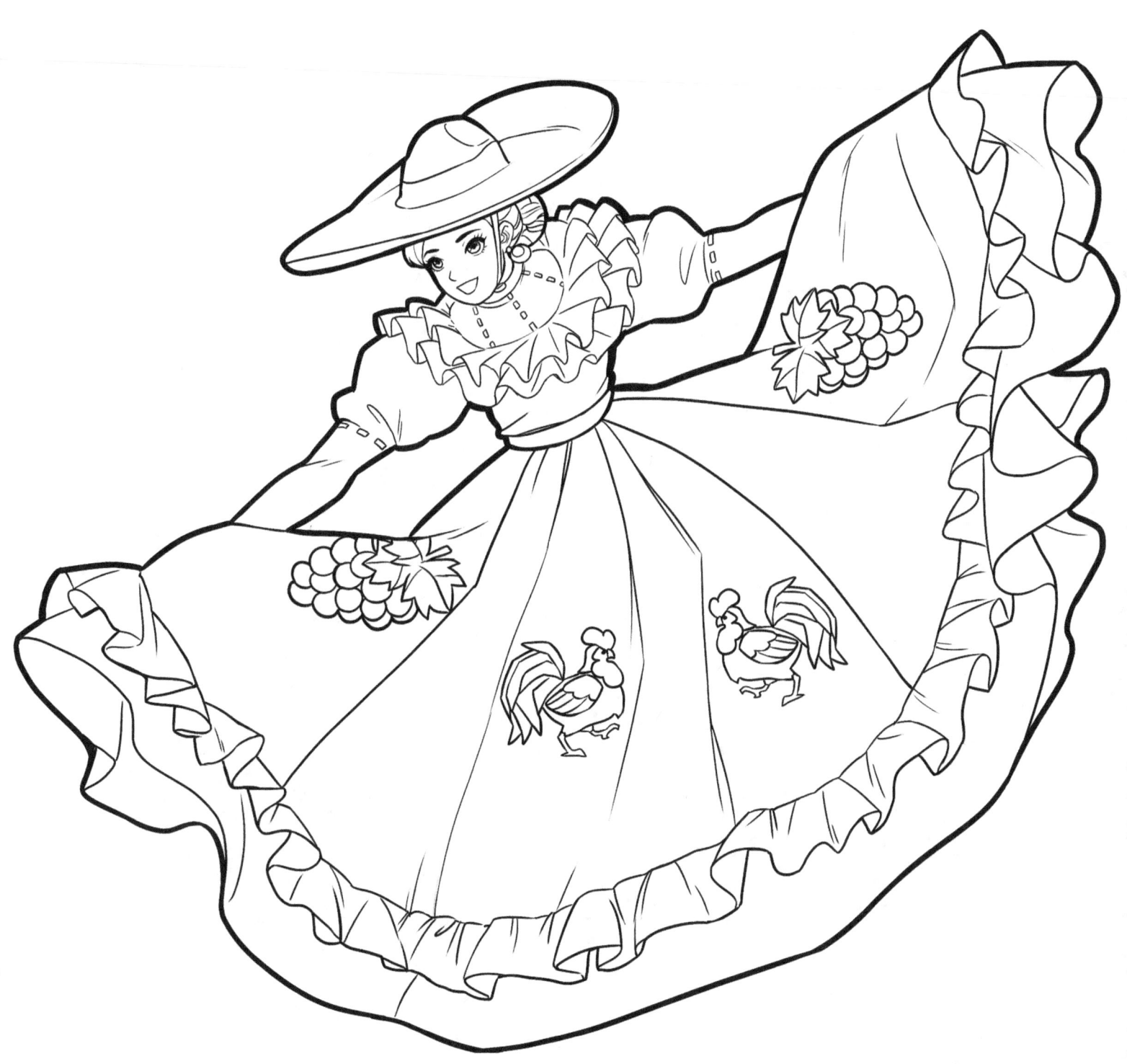

Aguascalientes

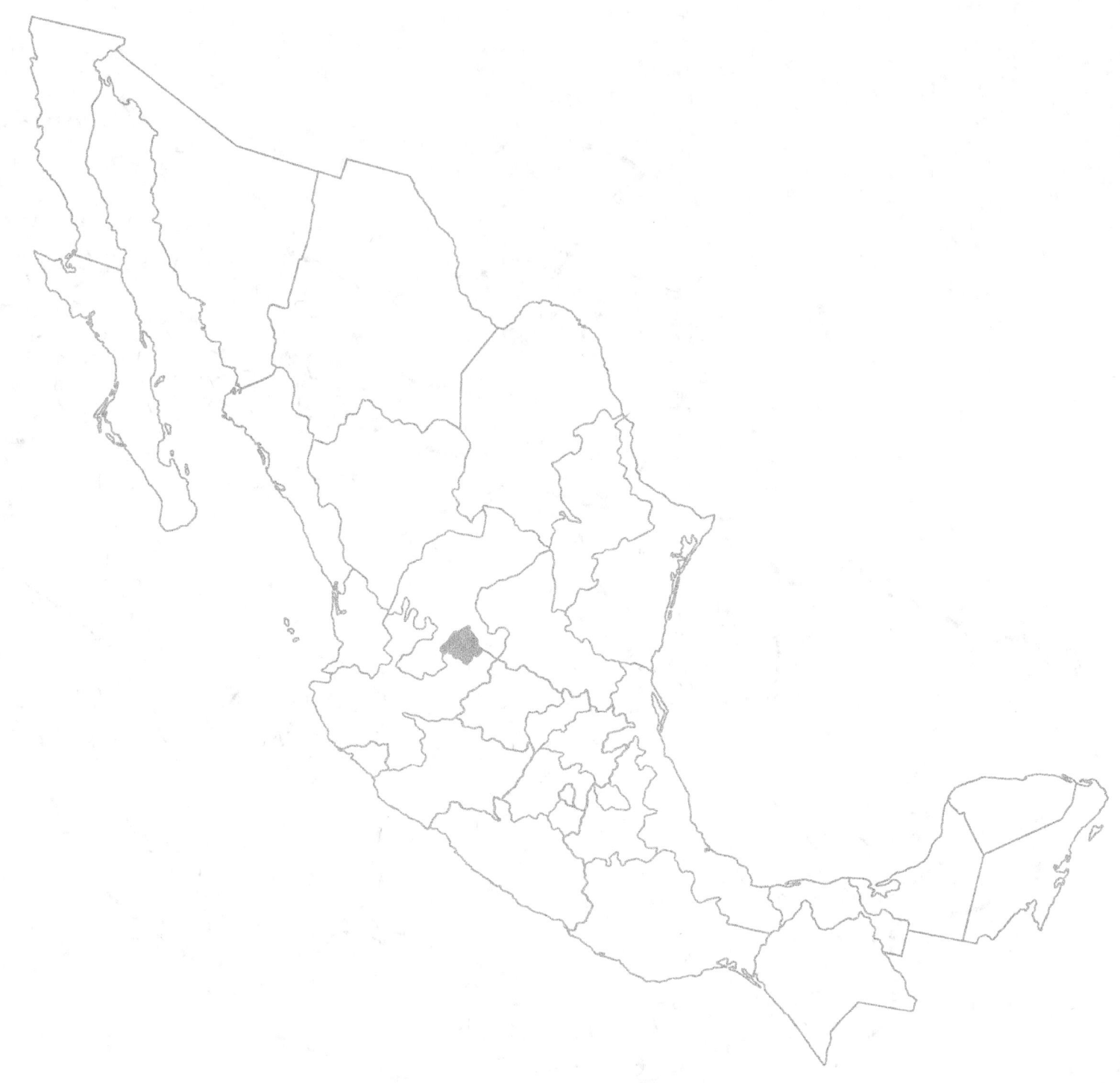

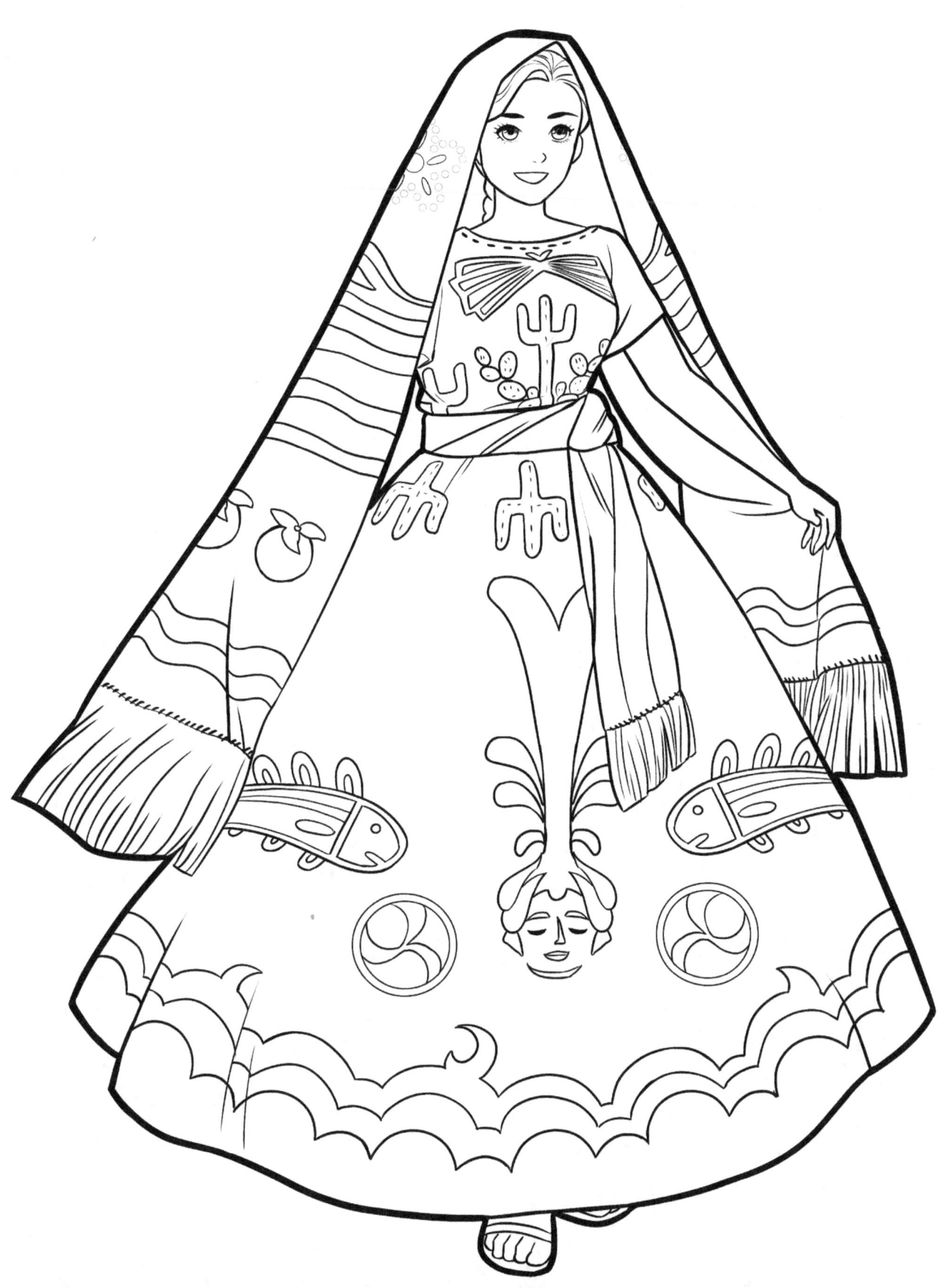

Baja California Norte

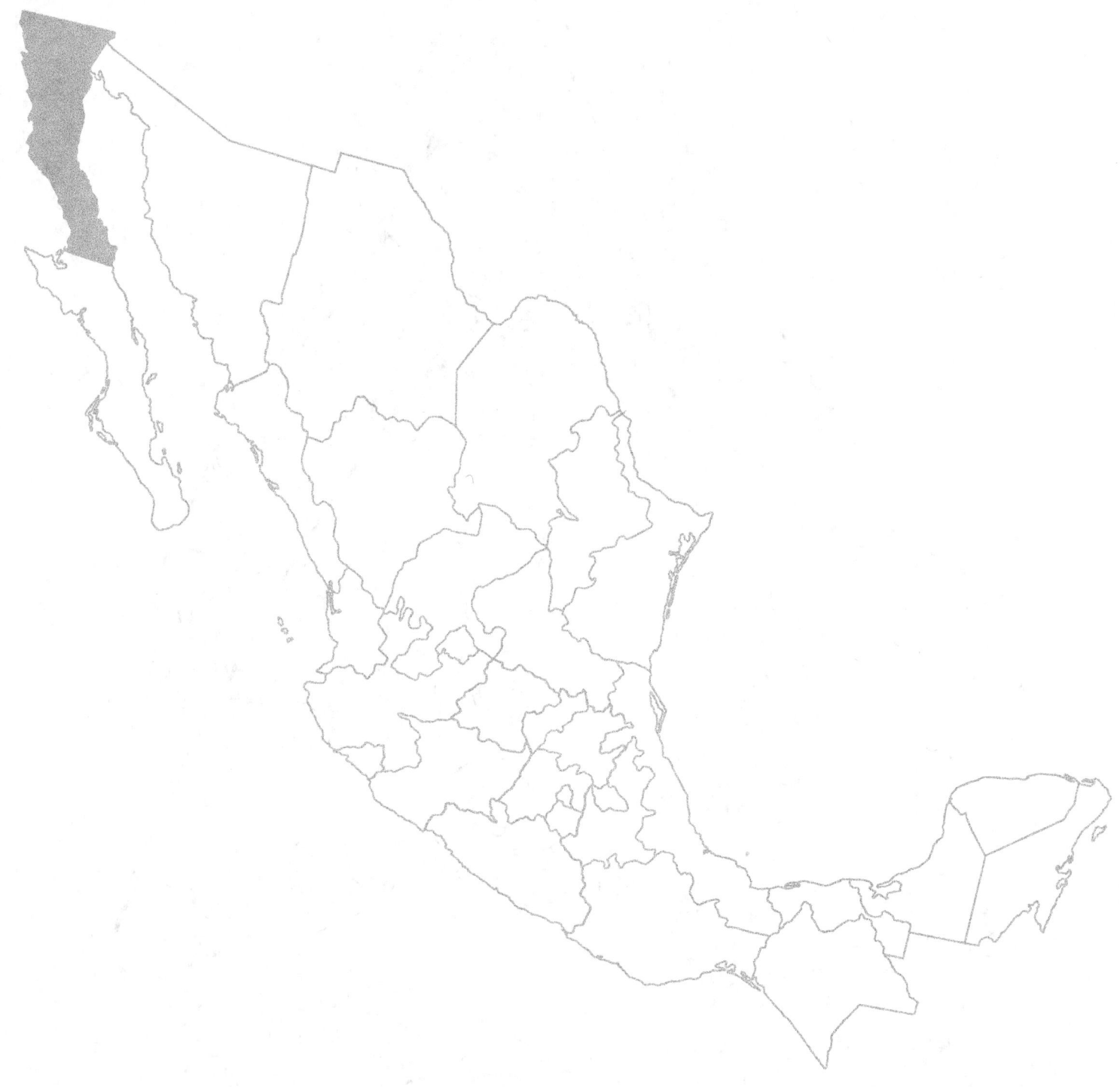

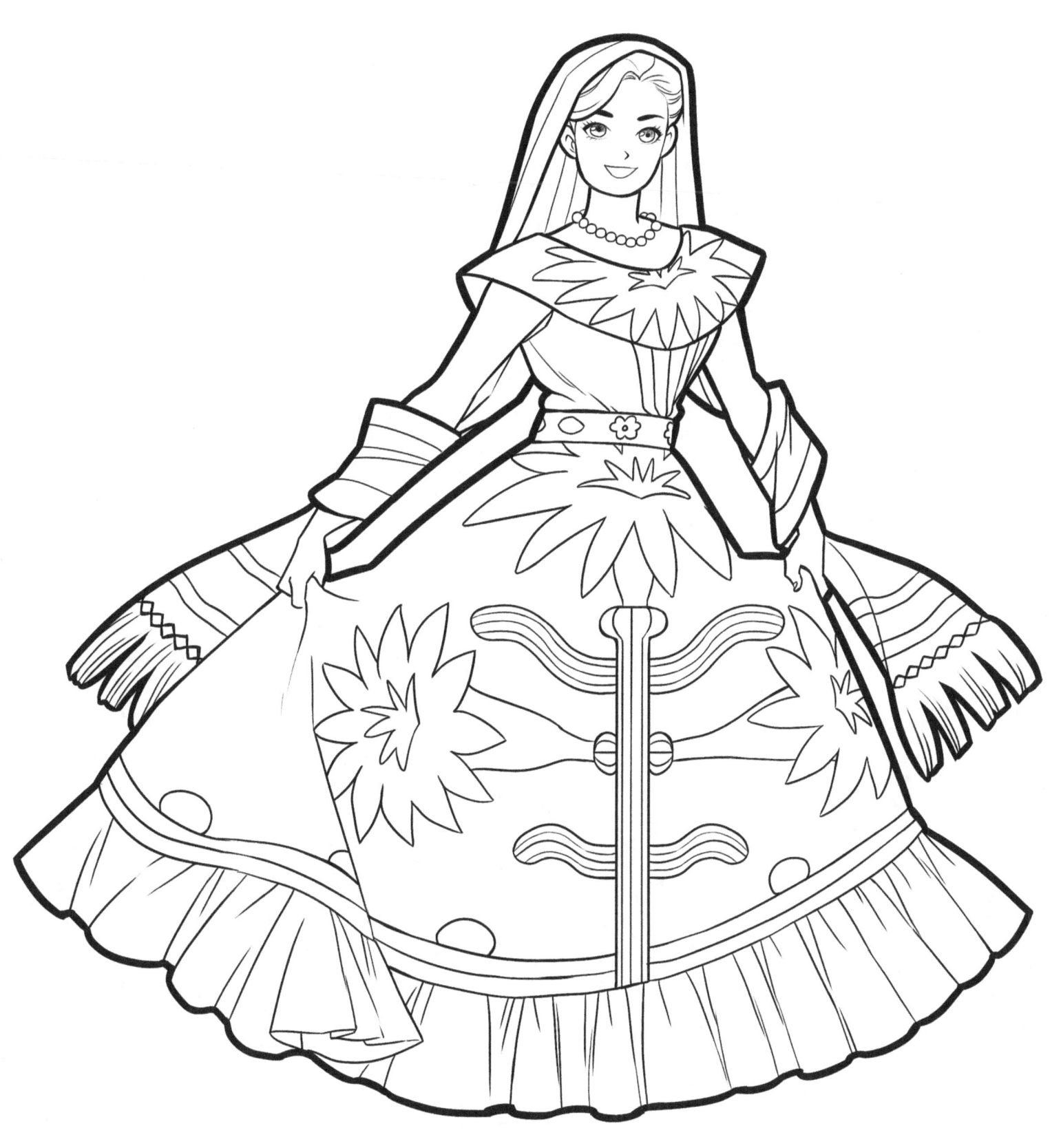

Baja California Sur

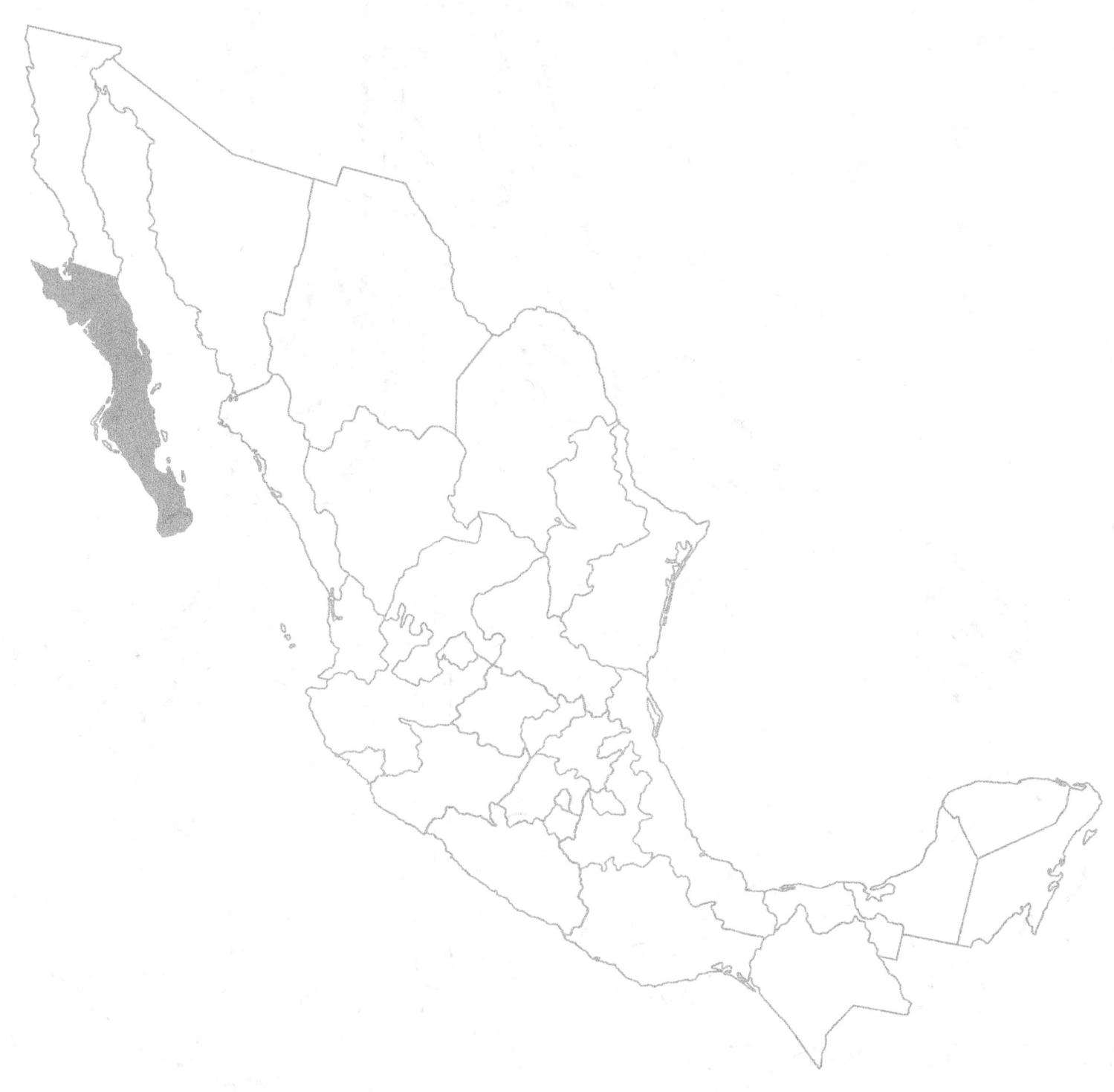

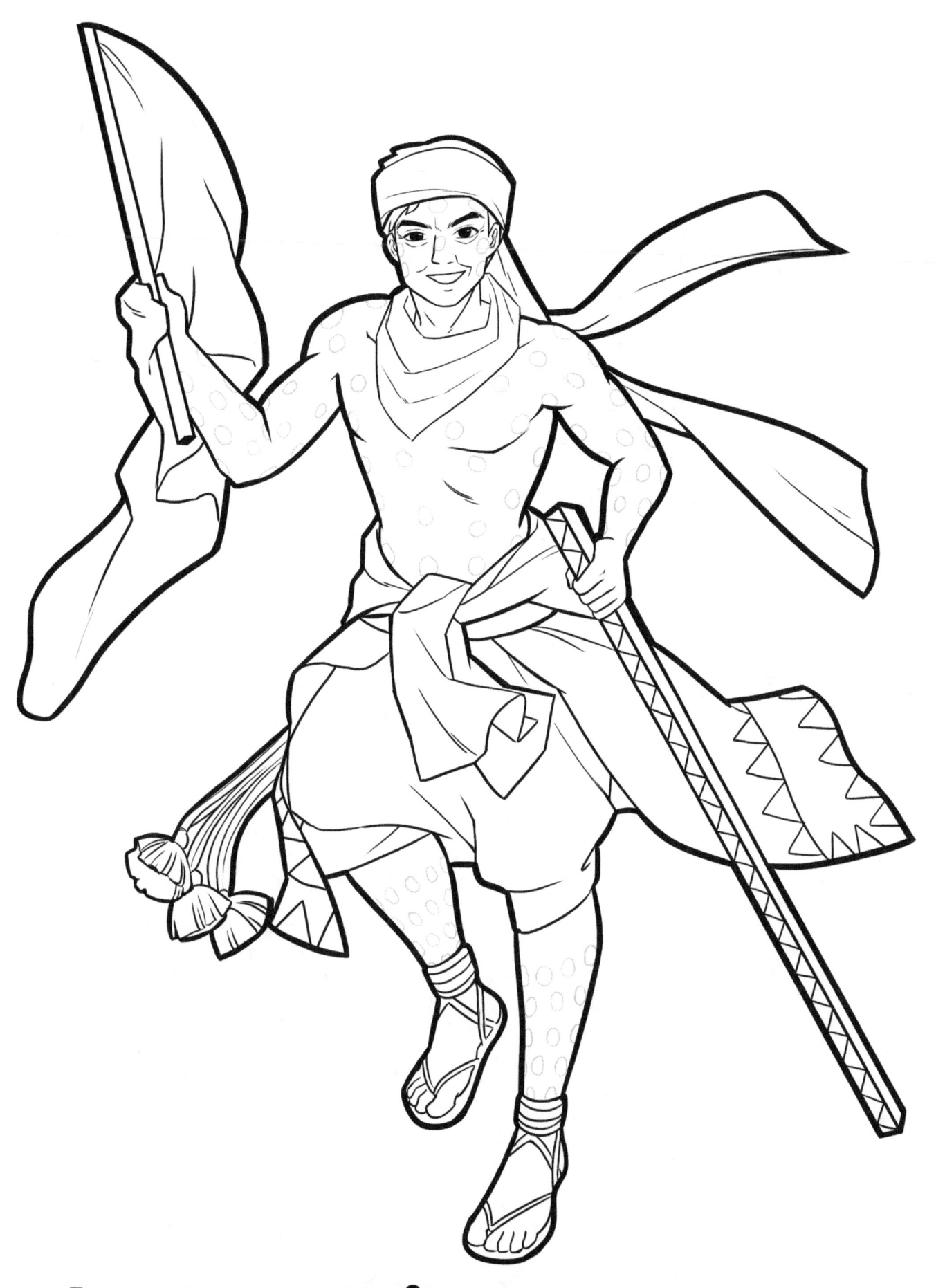

Tarahumara, Chihuahua

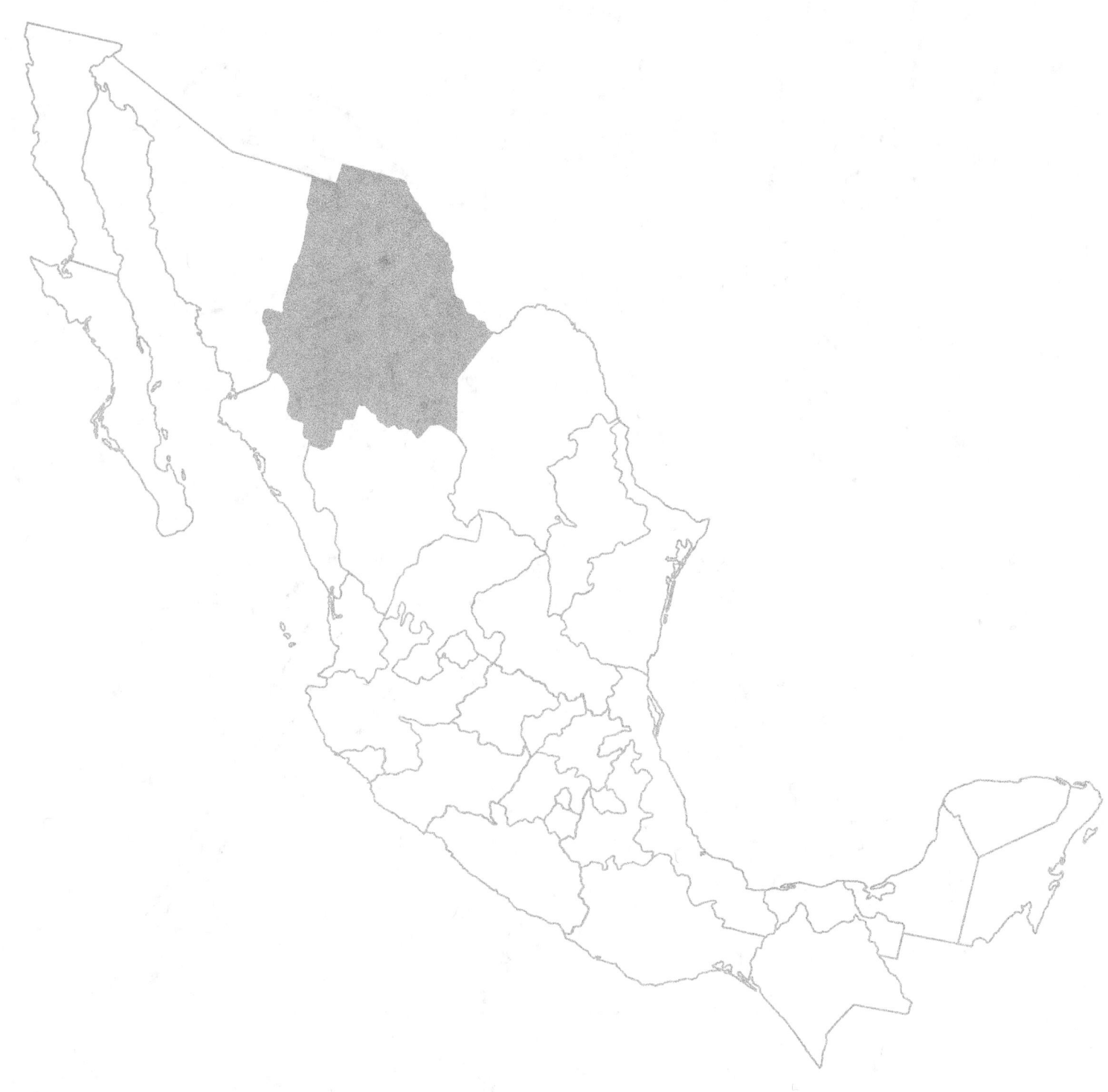

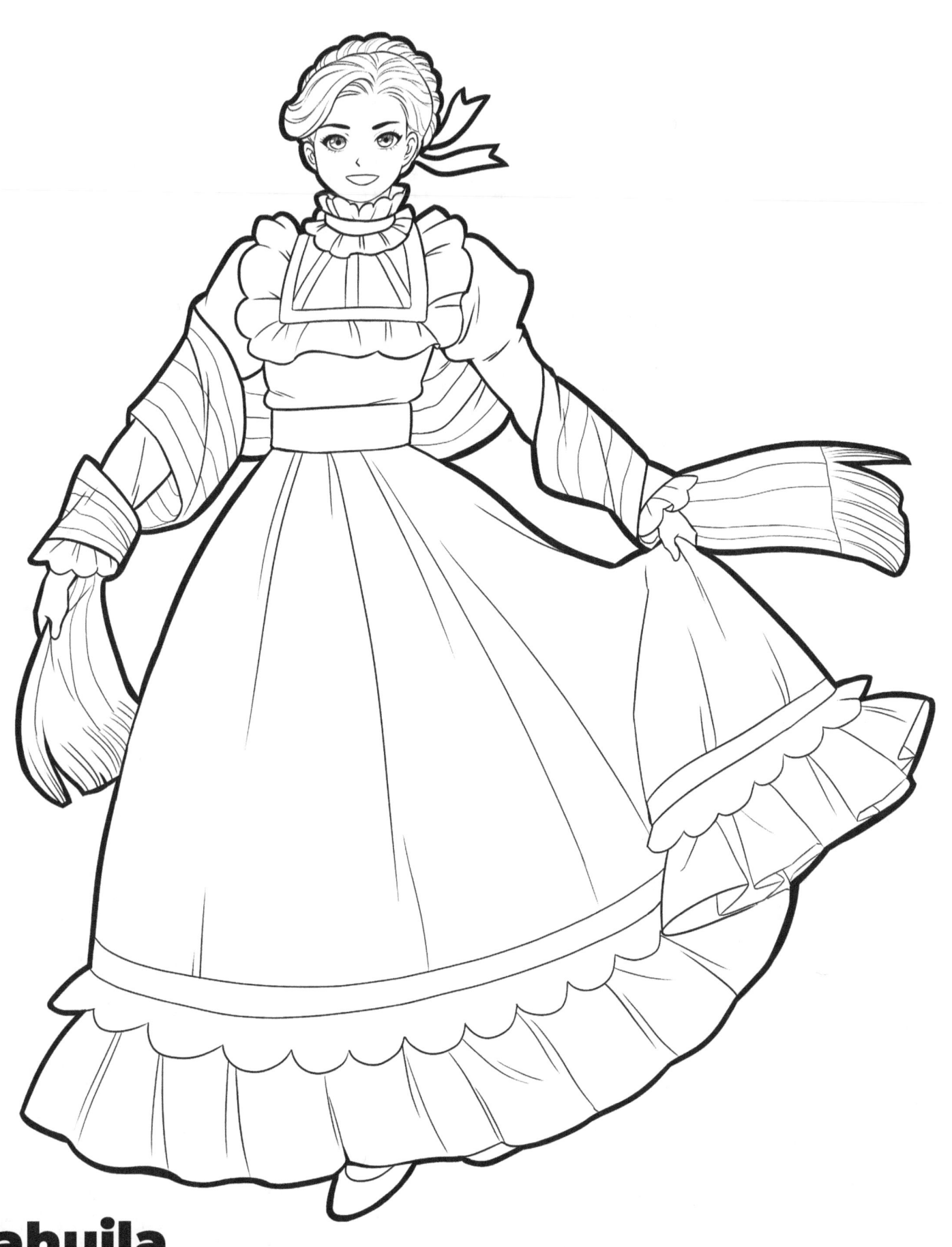

Coahuila

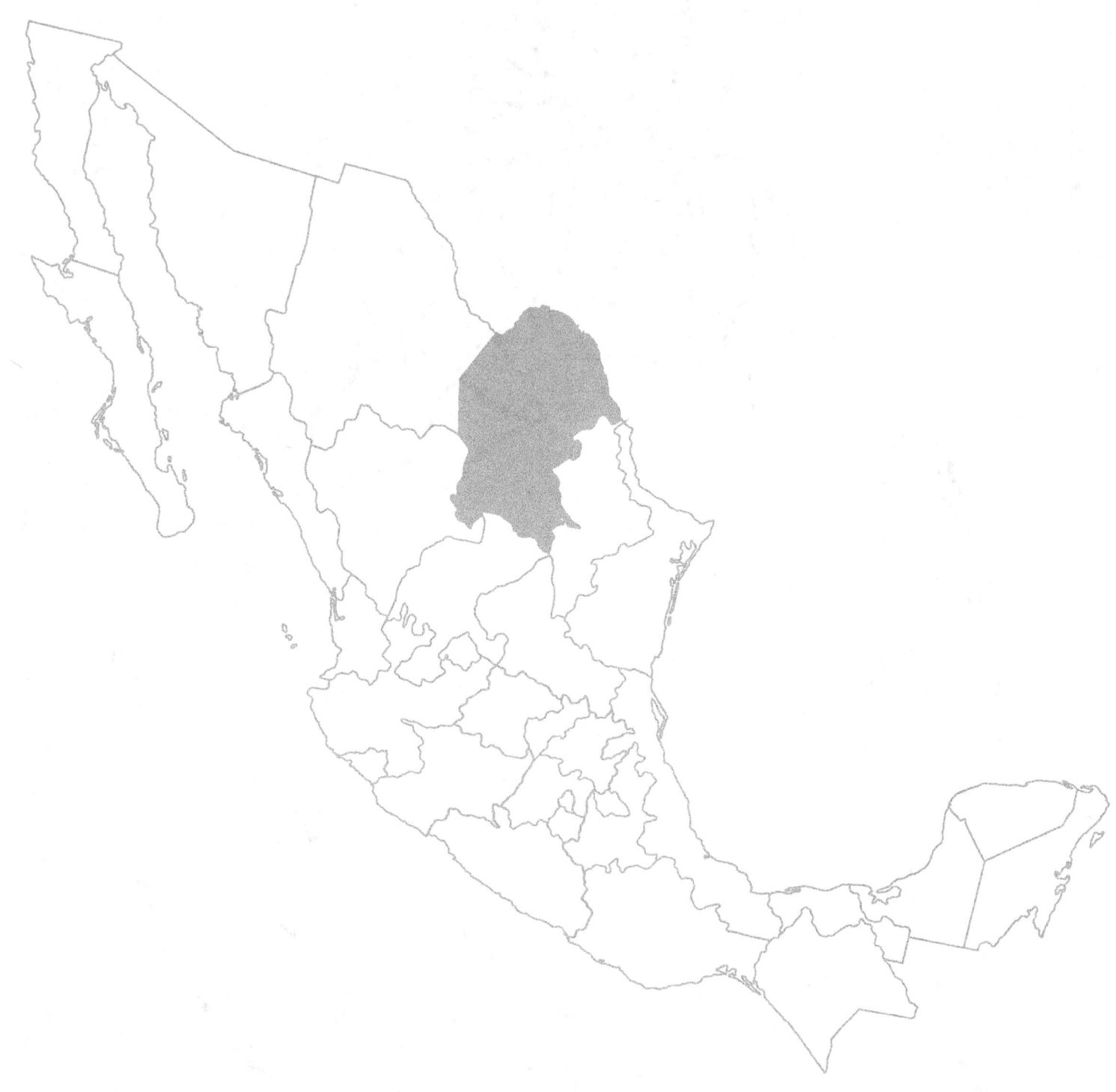

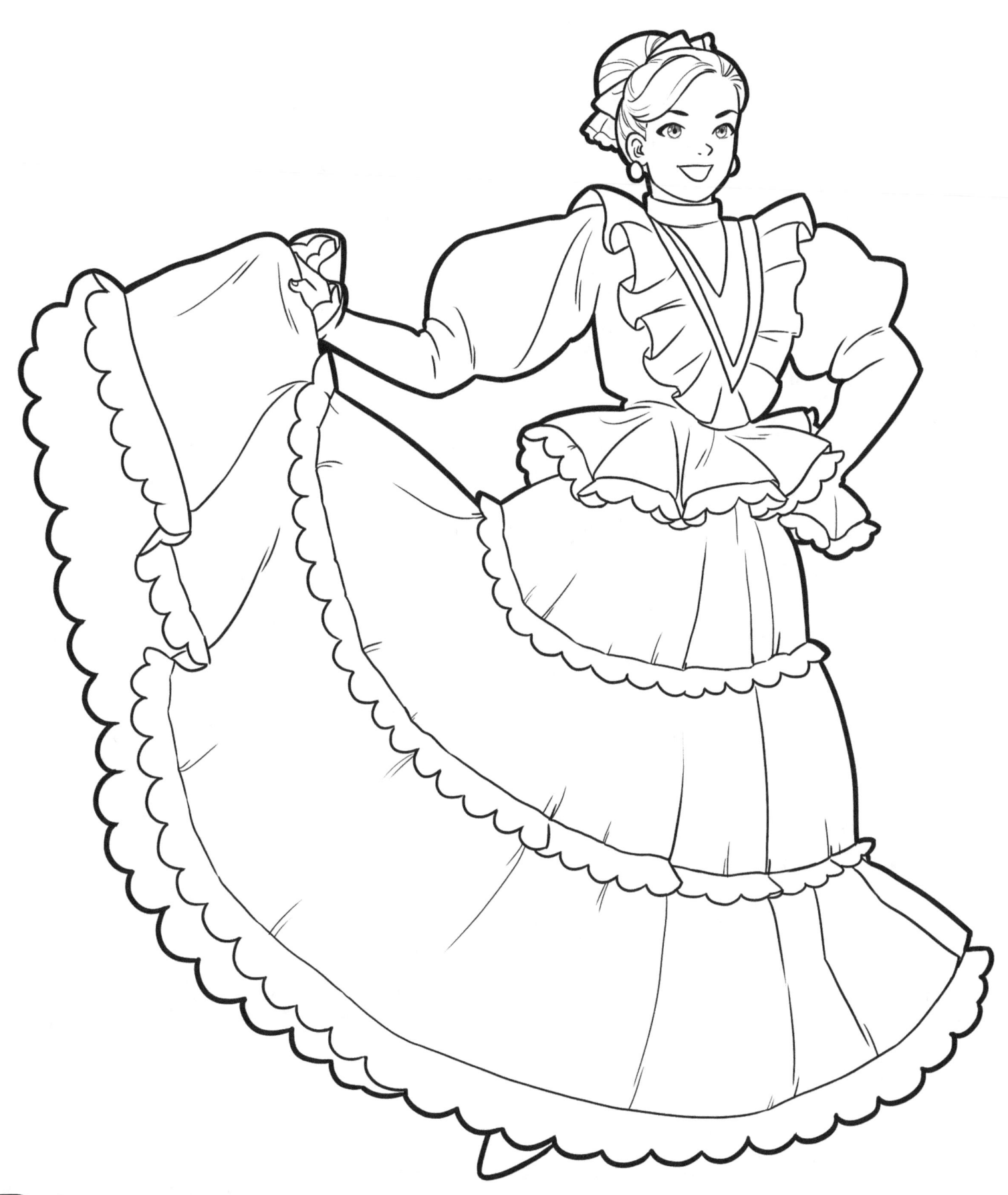

Durango

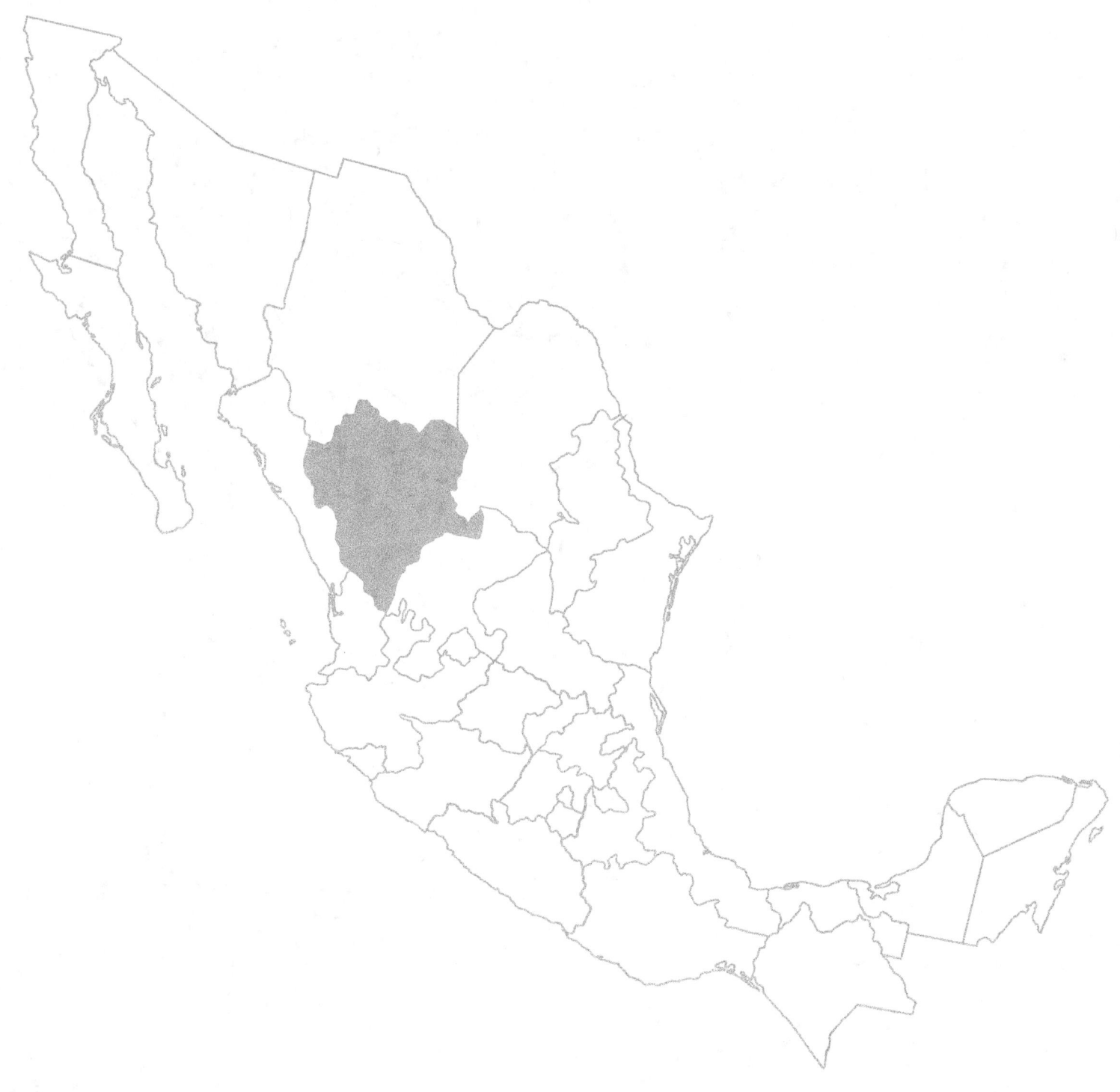

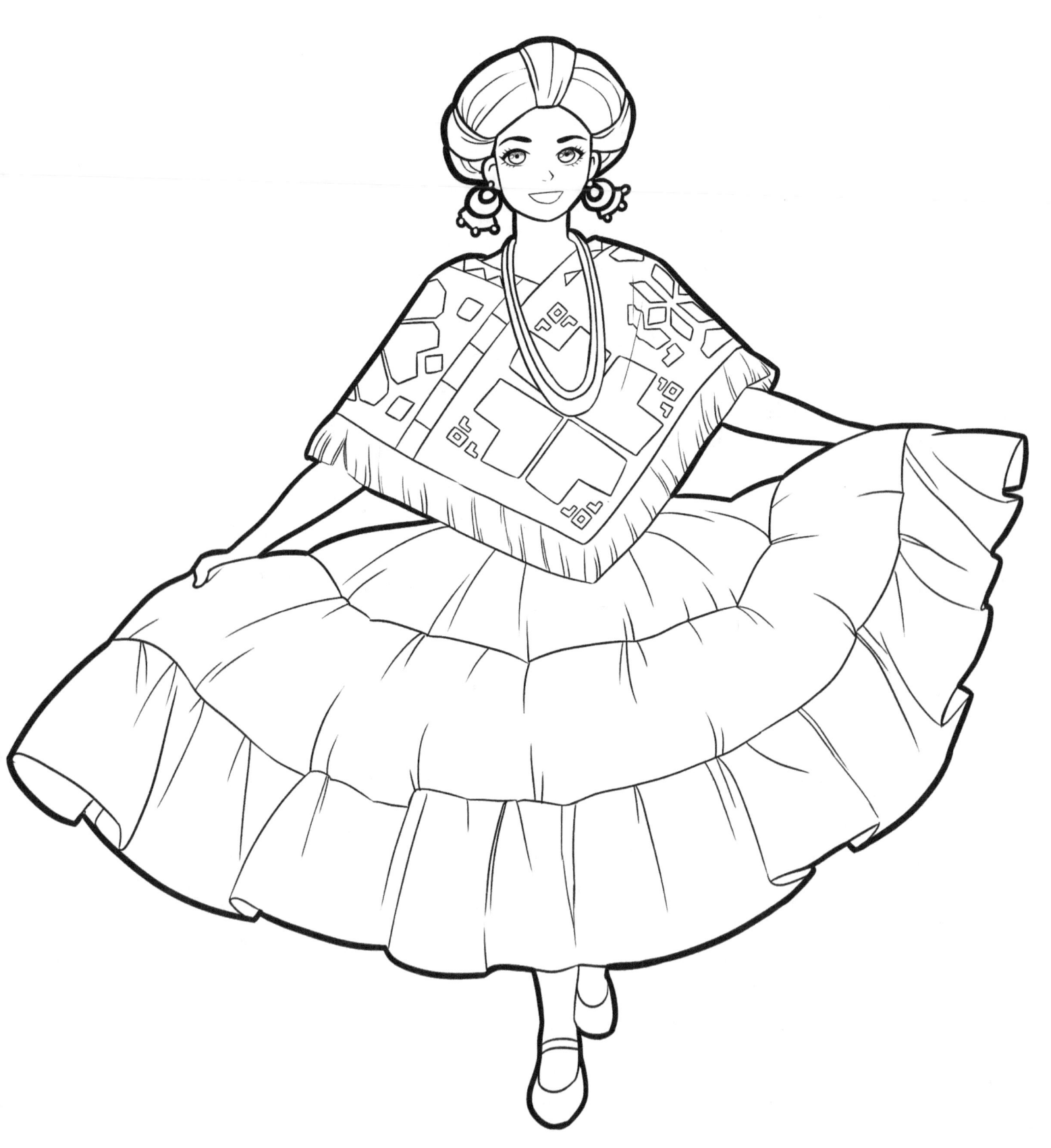

San Luis Potosí - Huasteca

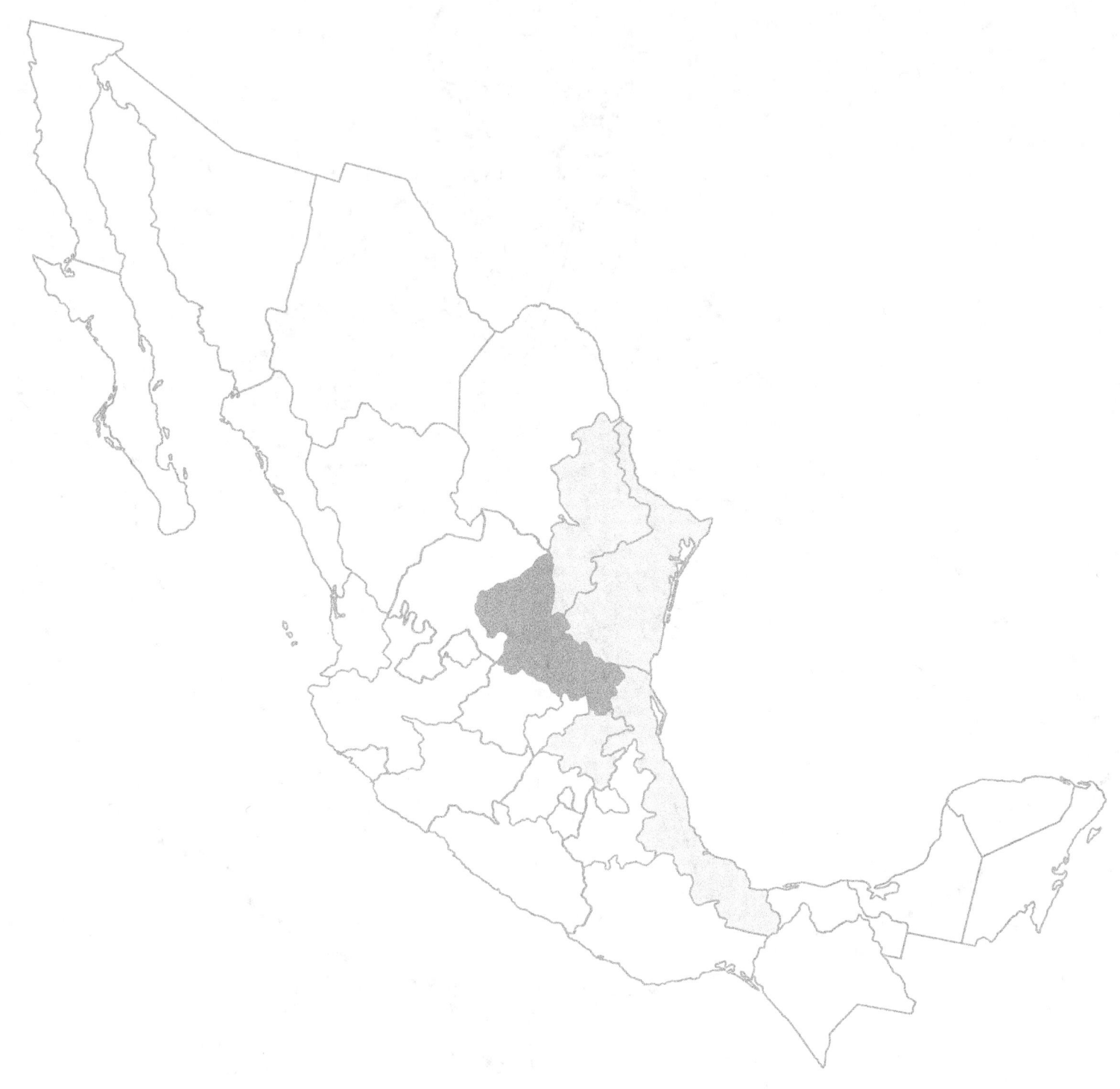

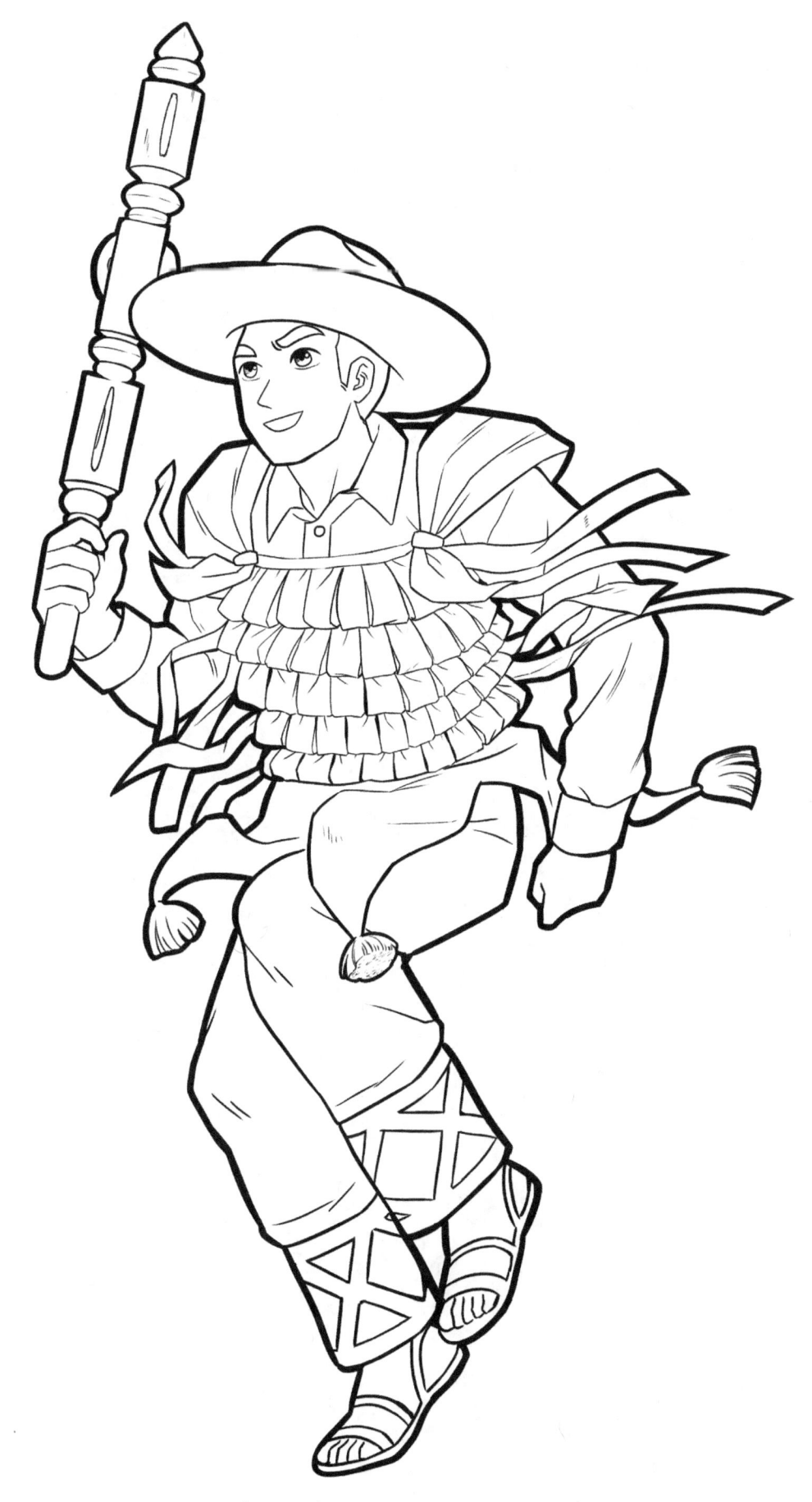

Jalisco Danza de los Sonajeros

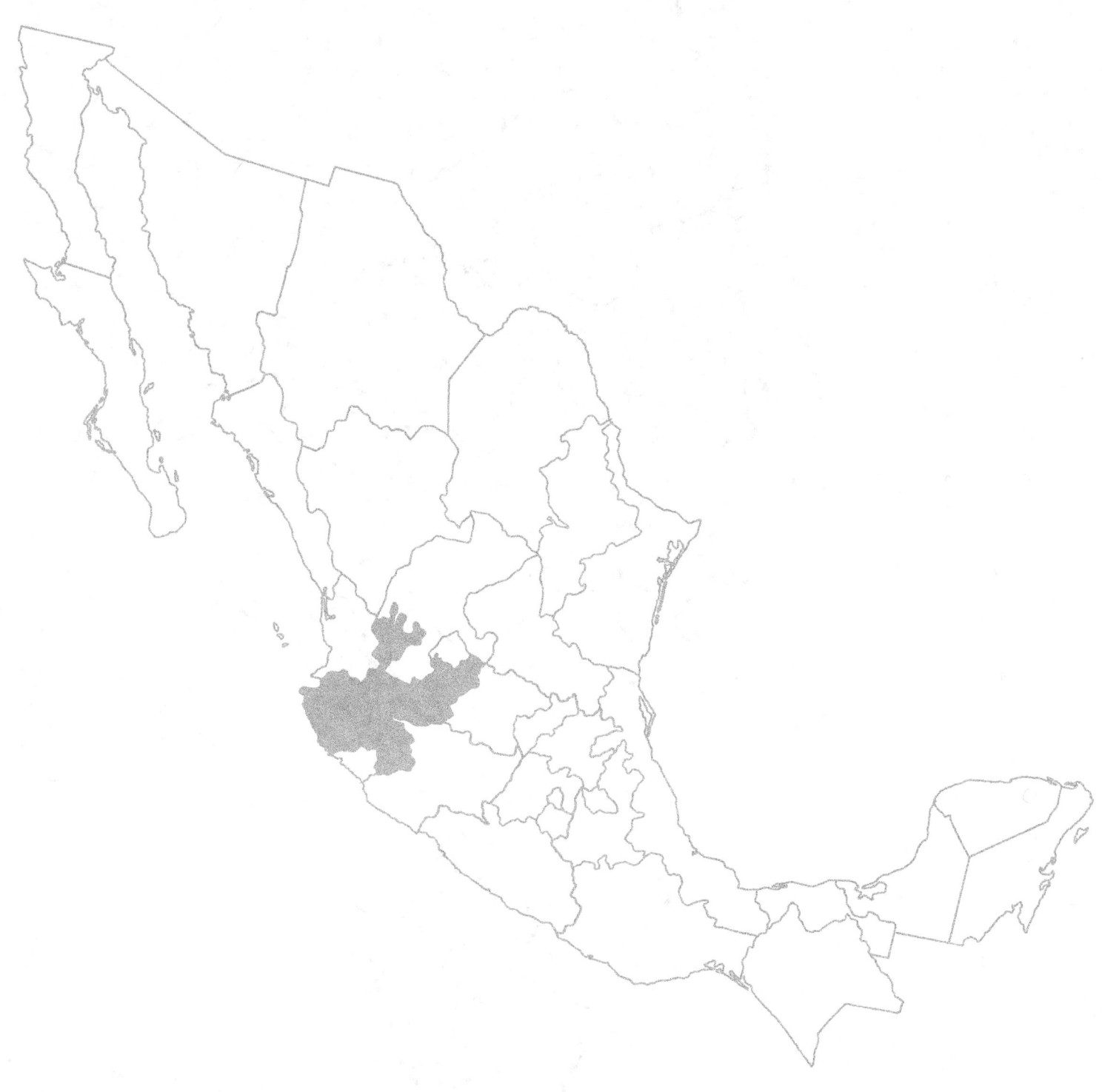

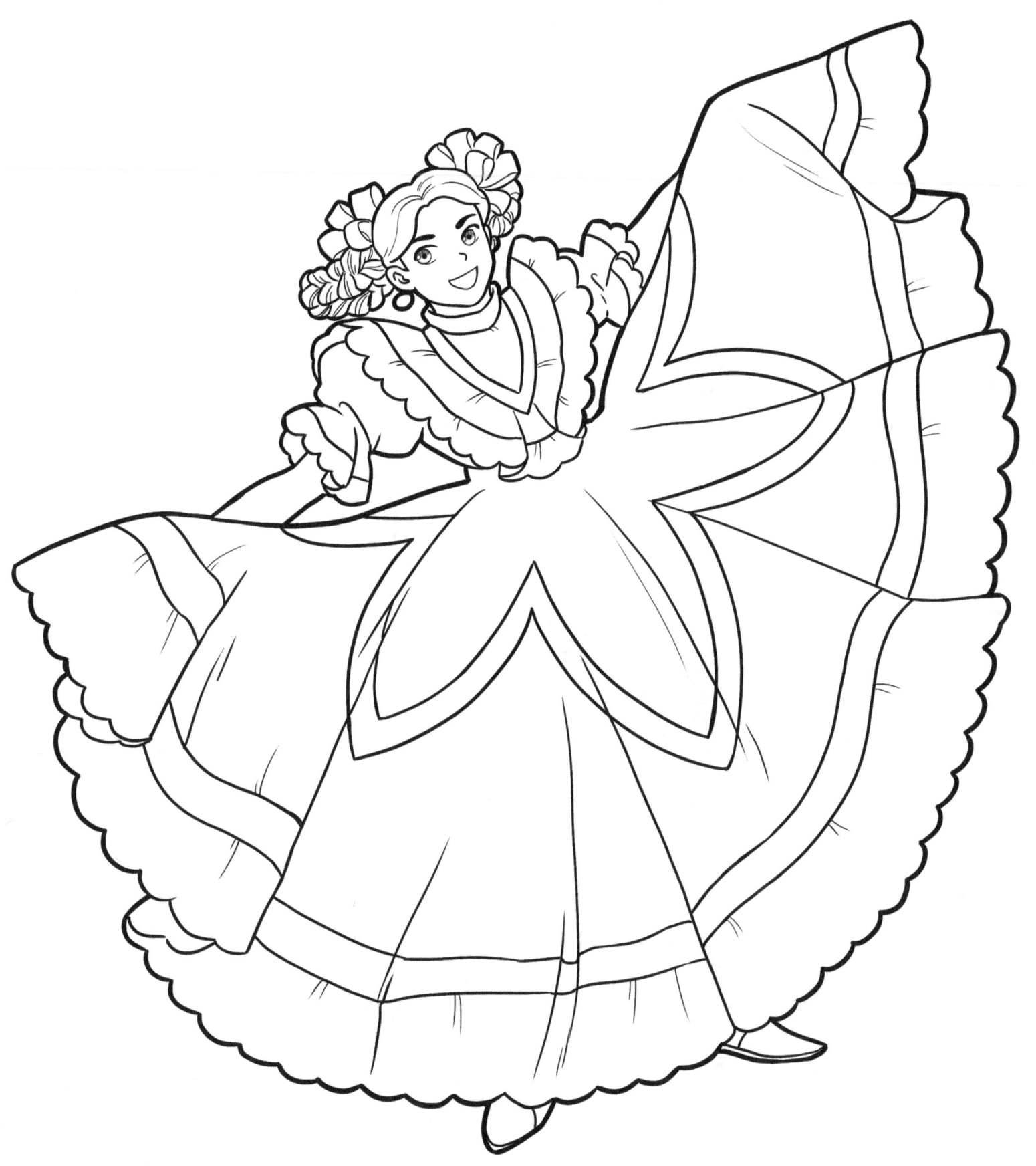

Jalisco

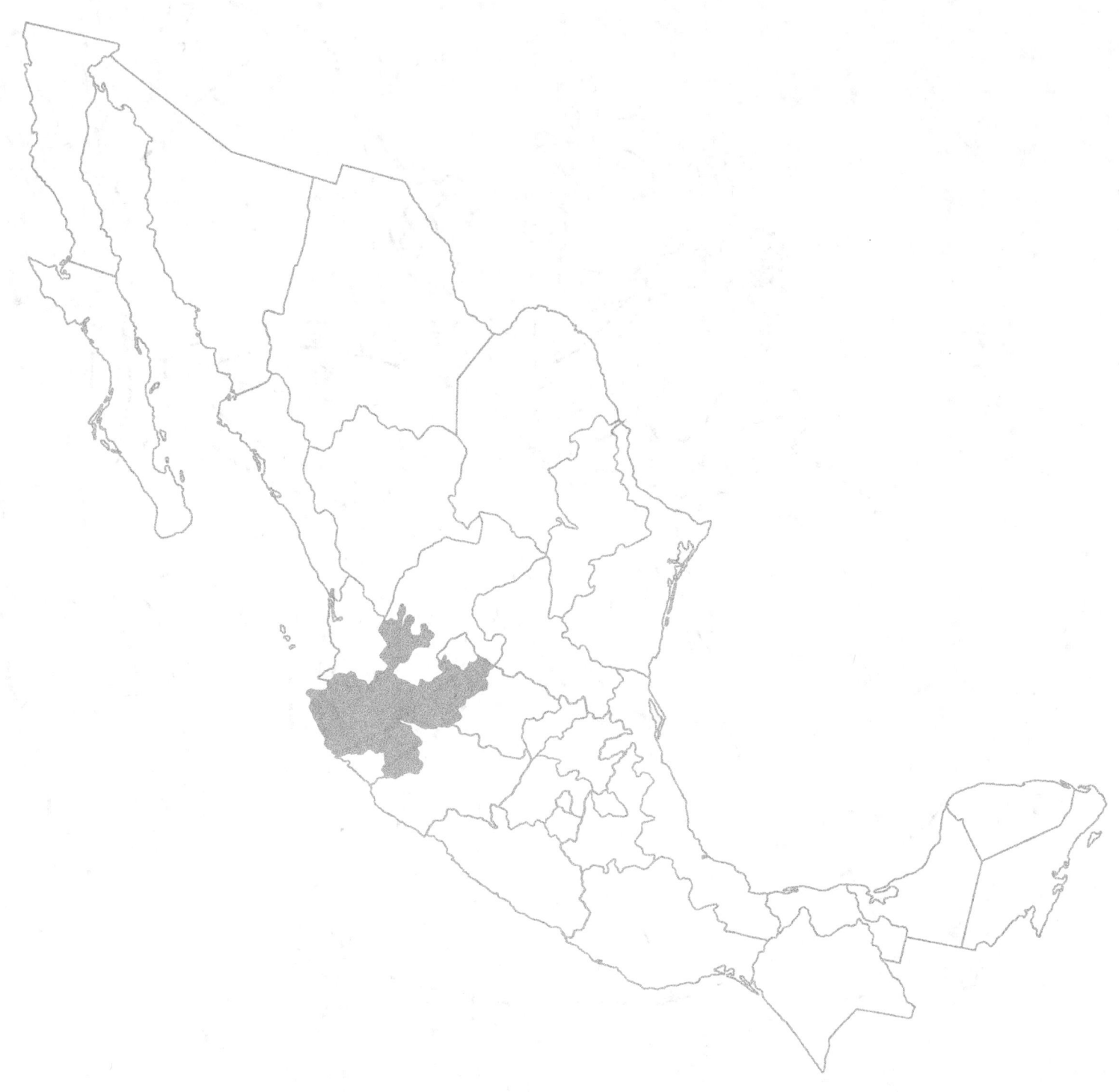

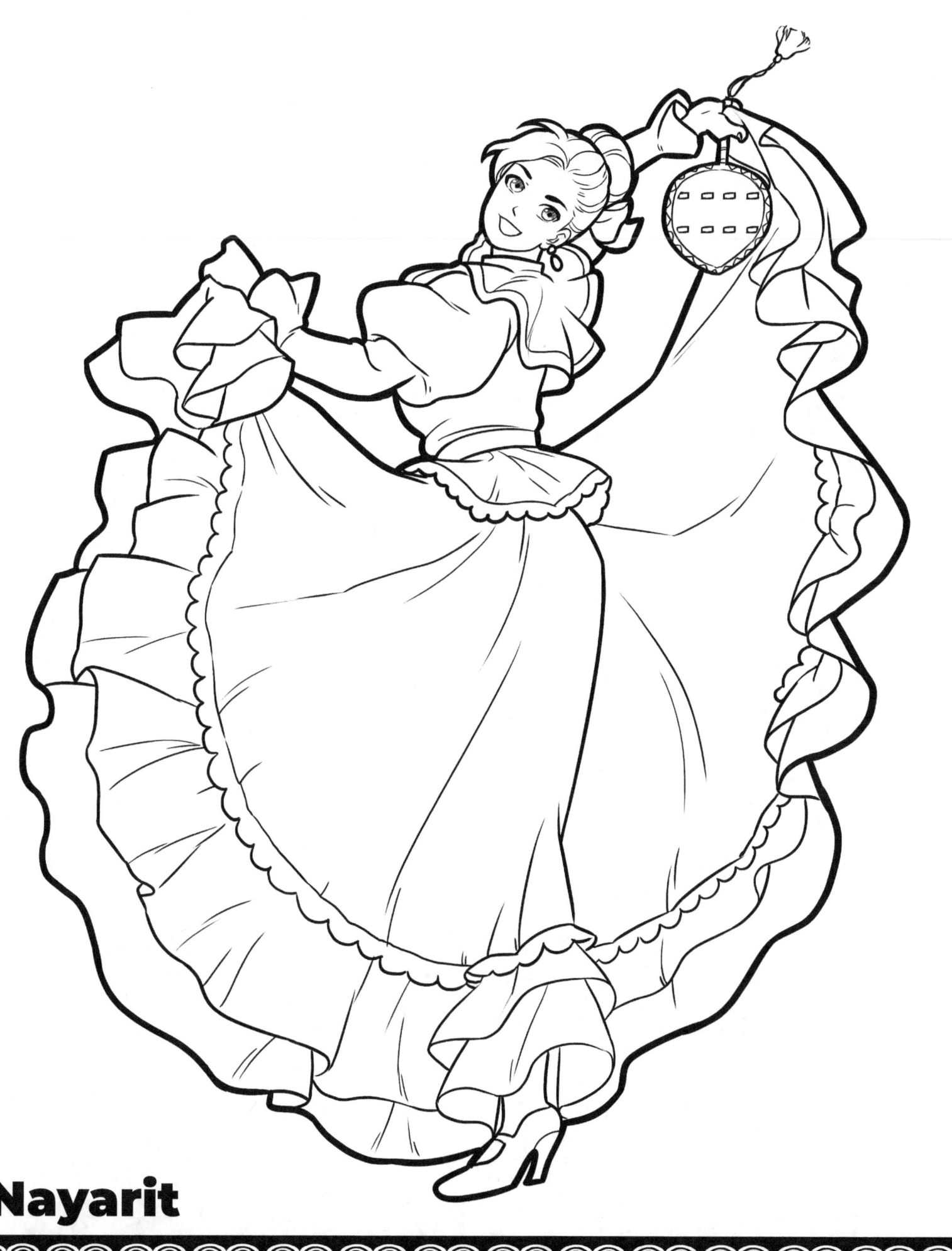

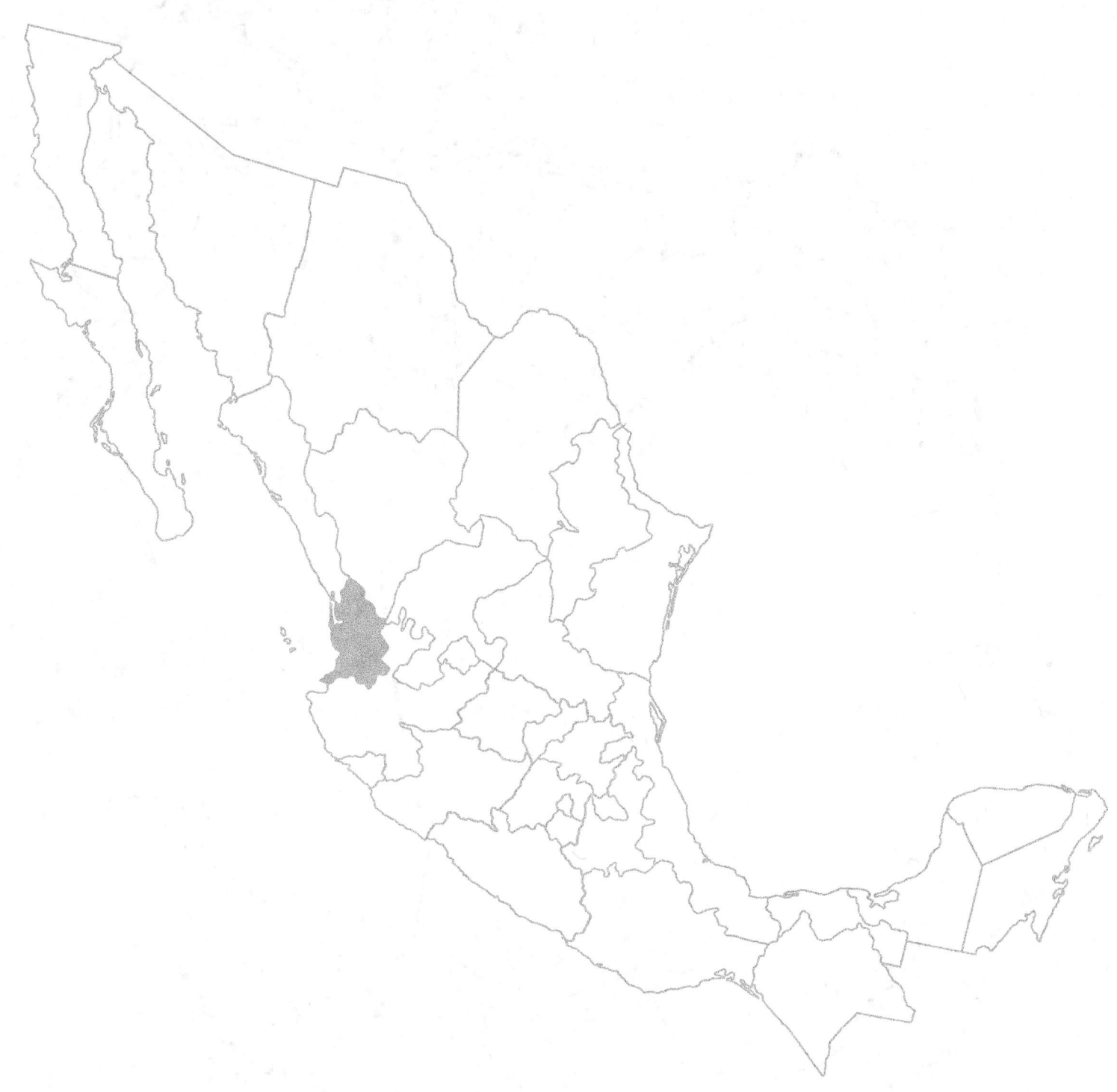

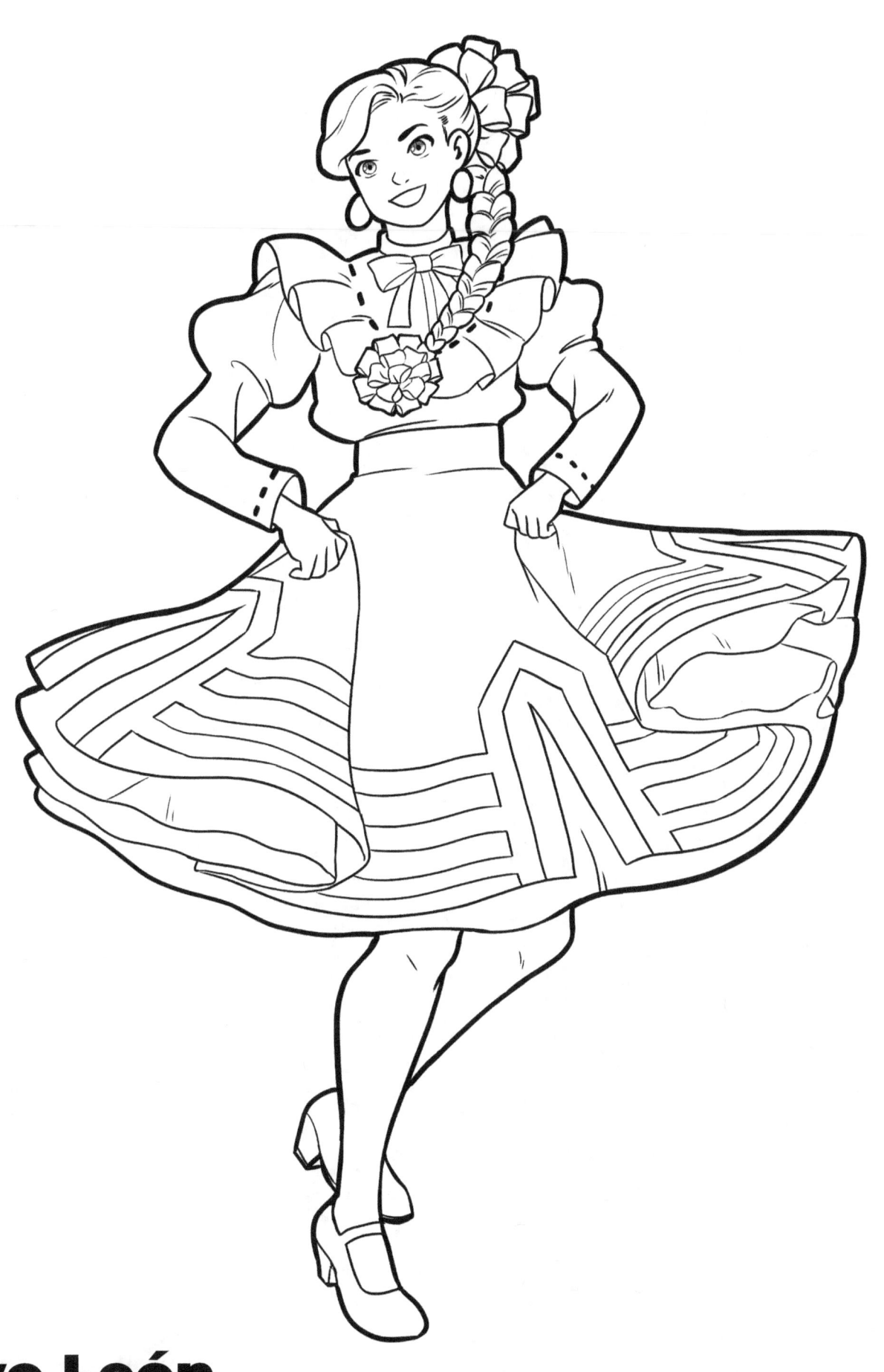

Nuevo León

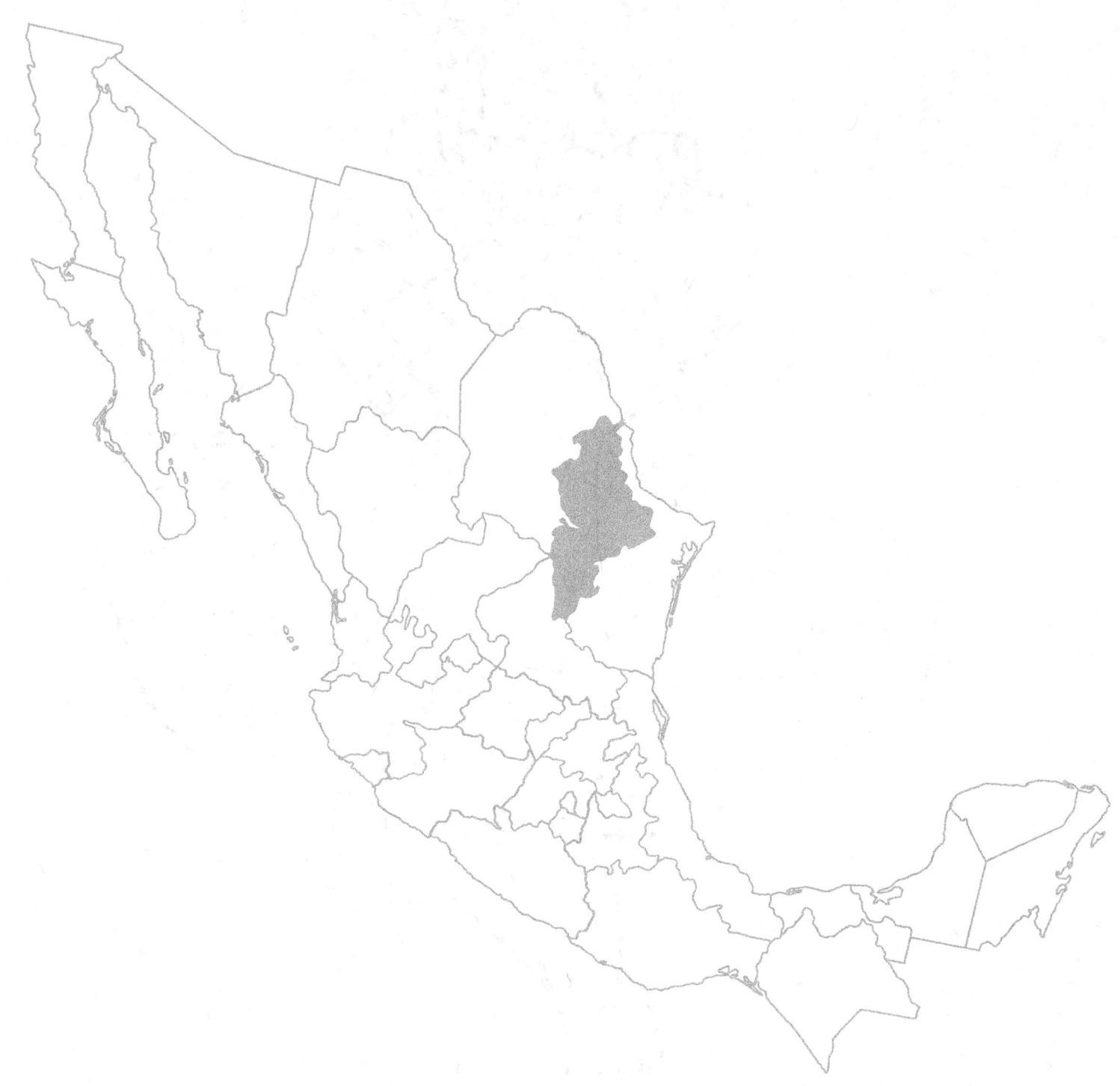

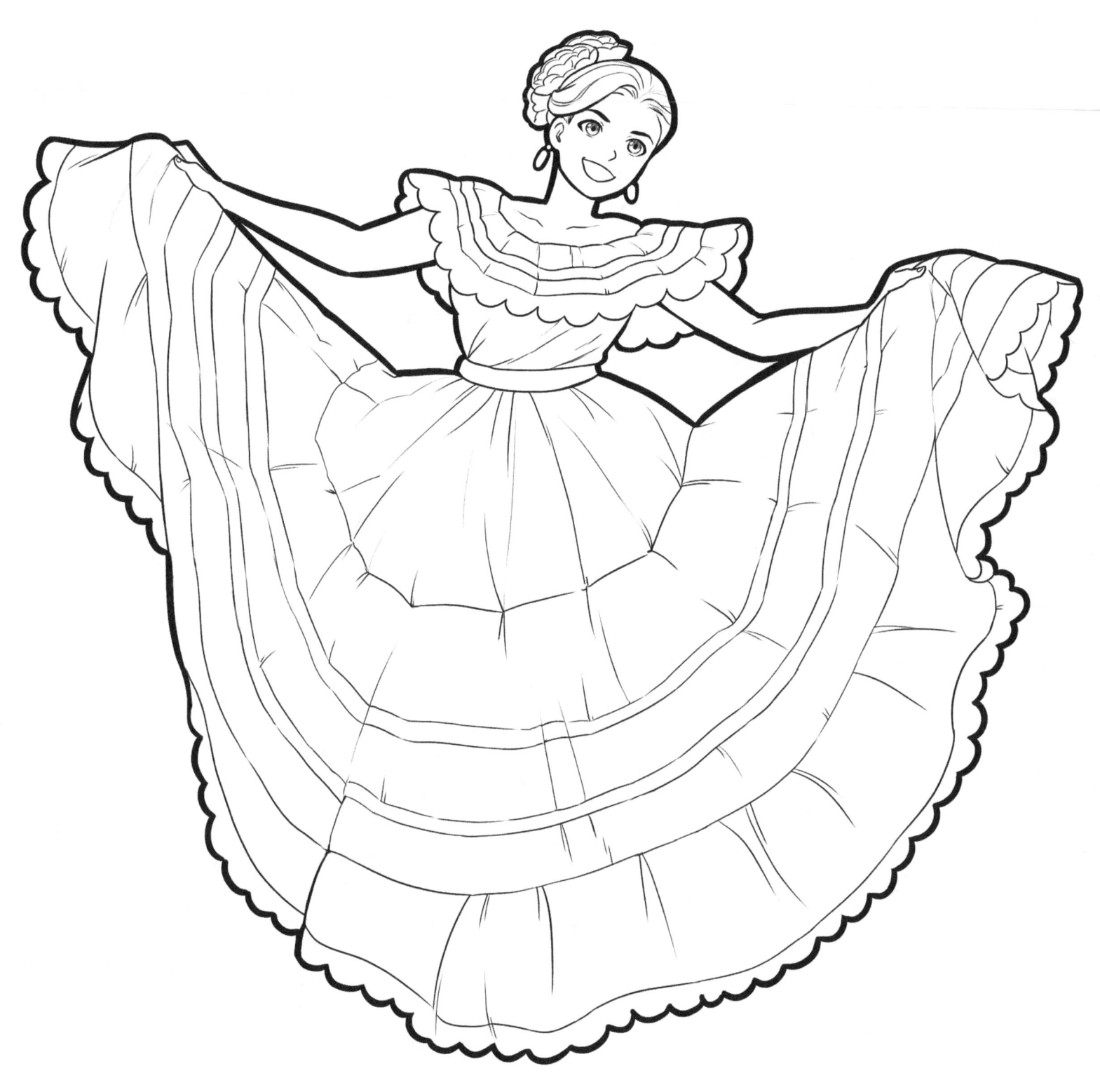

Sinaloa

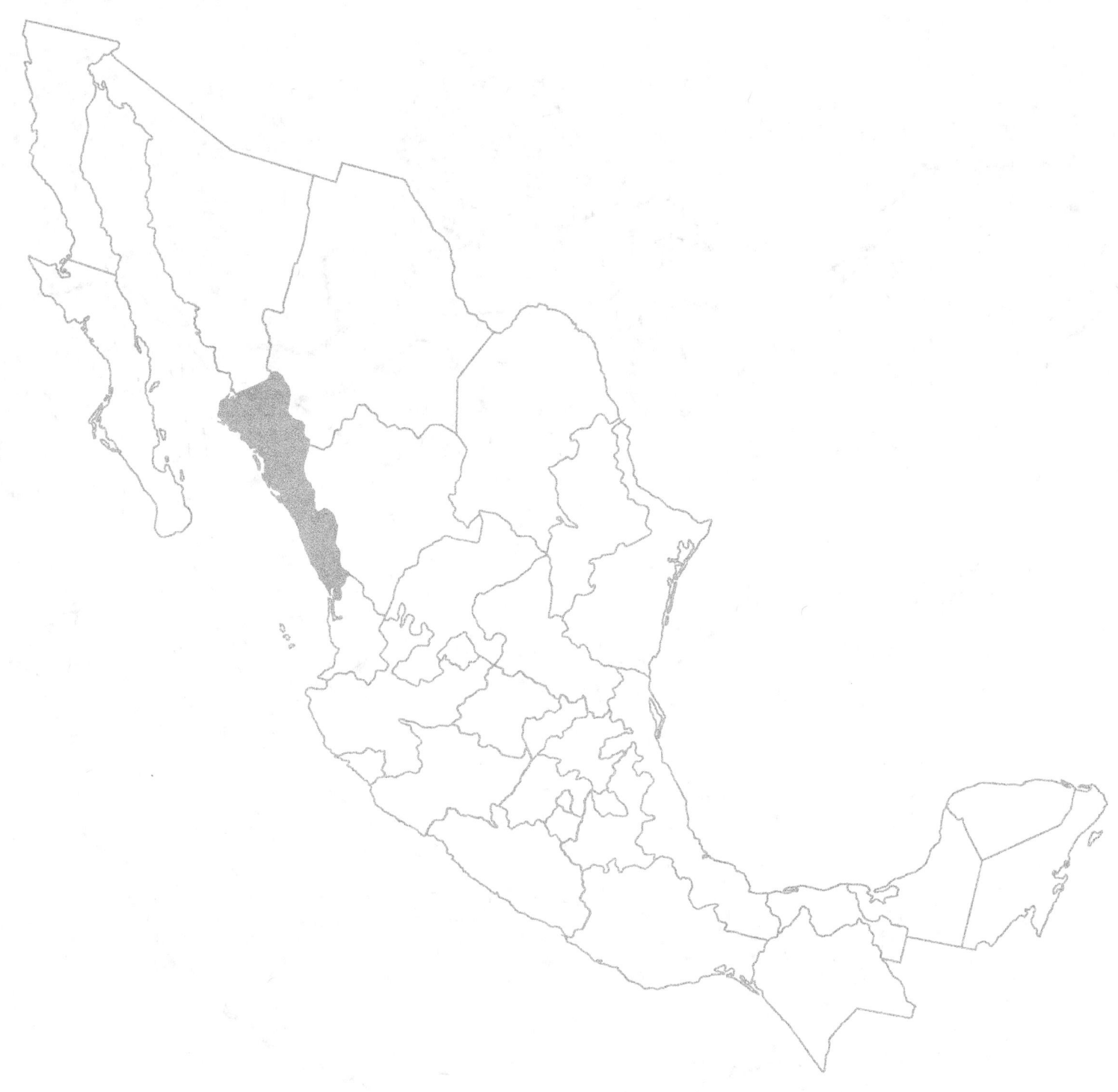

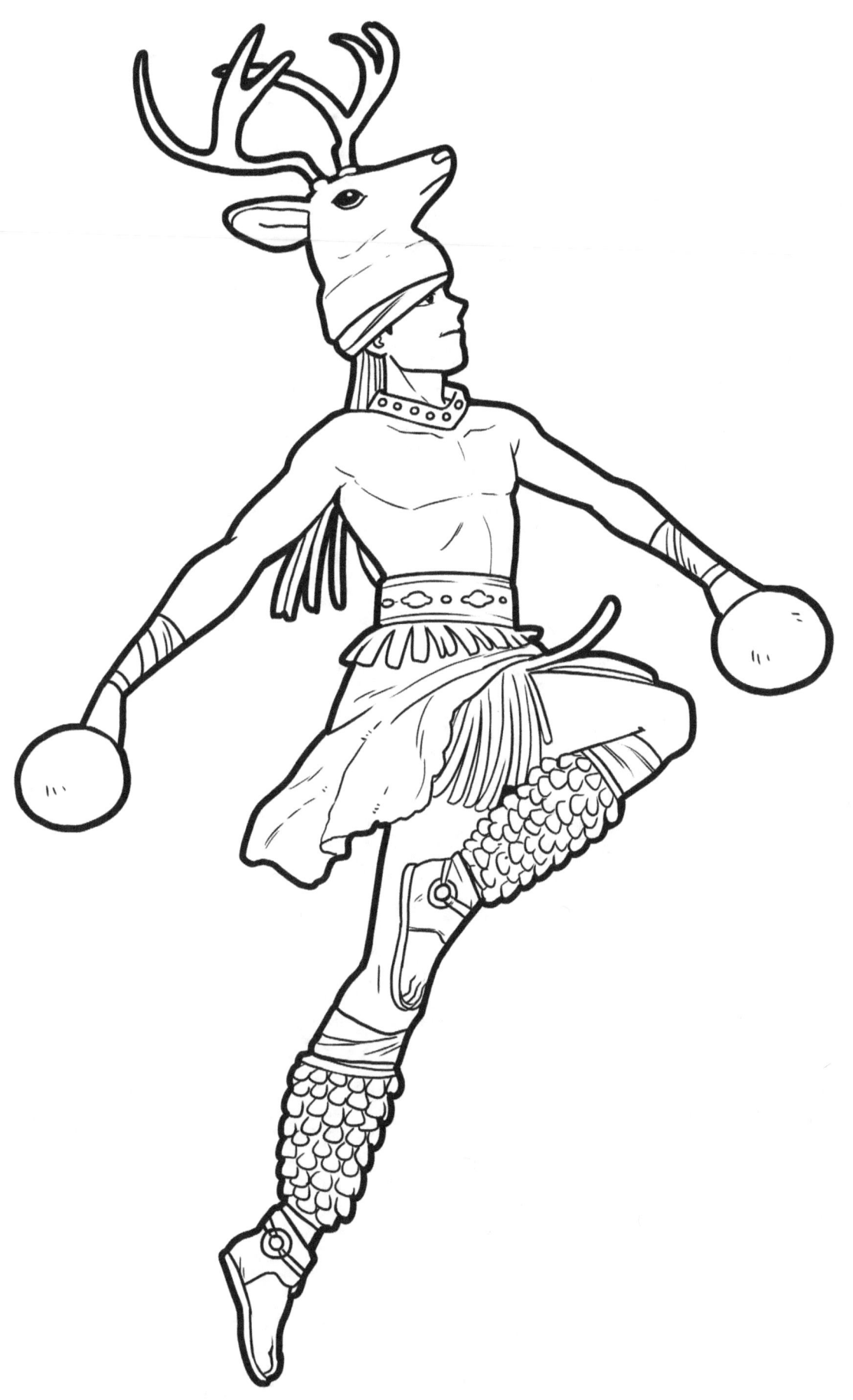

Sonora La Danza del Venado

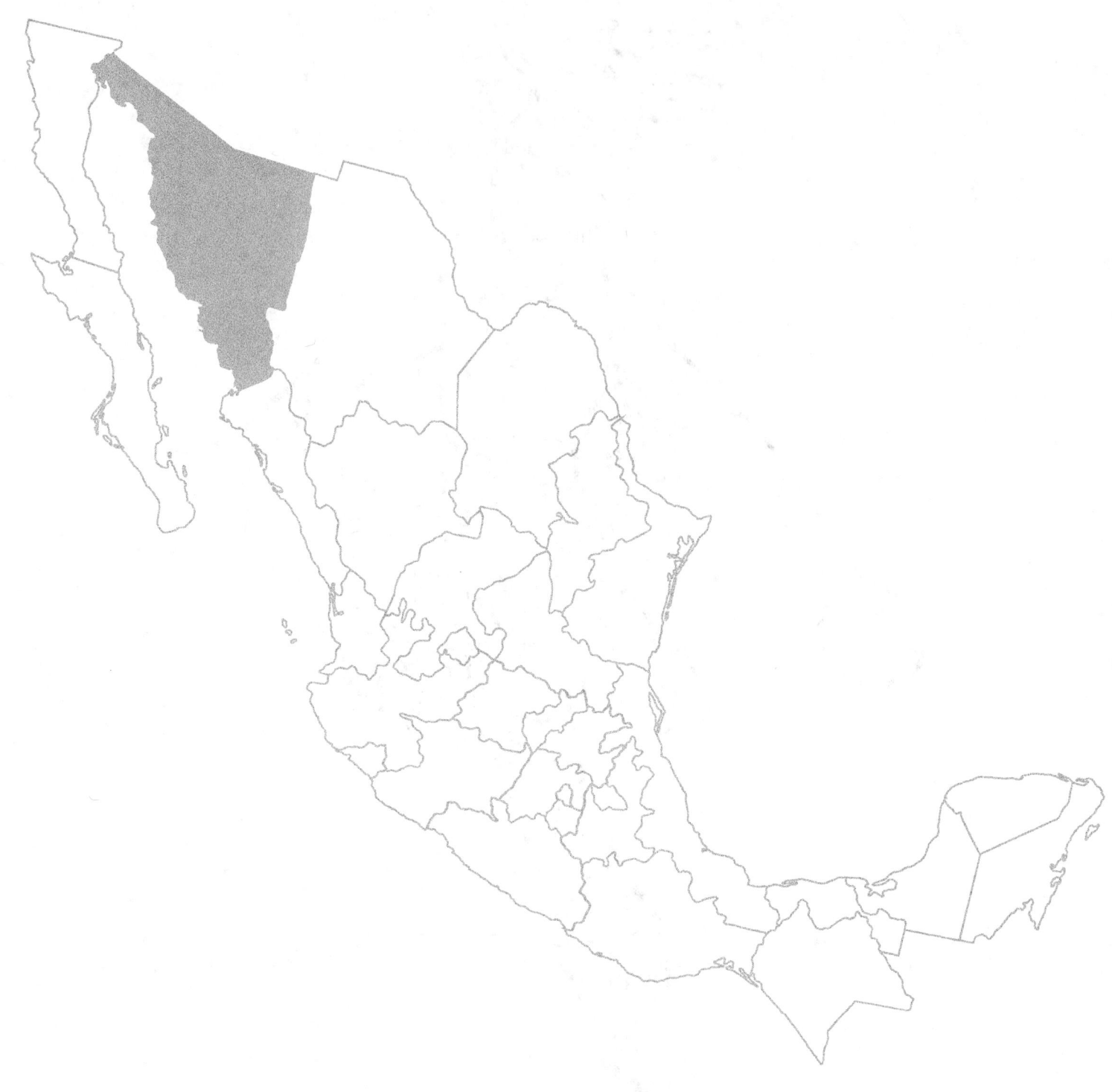

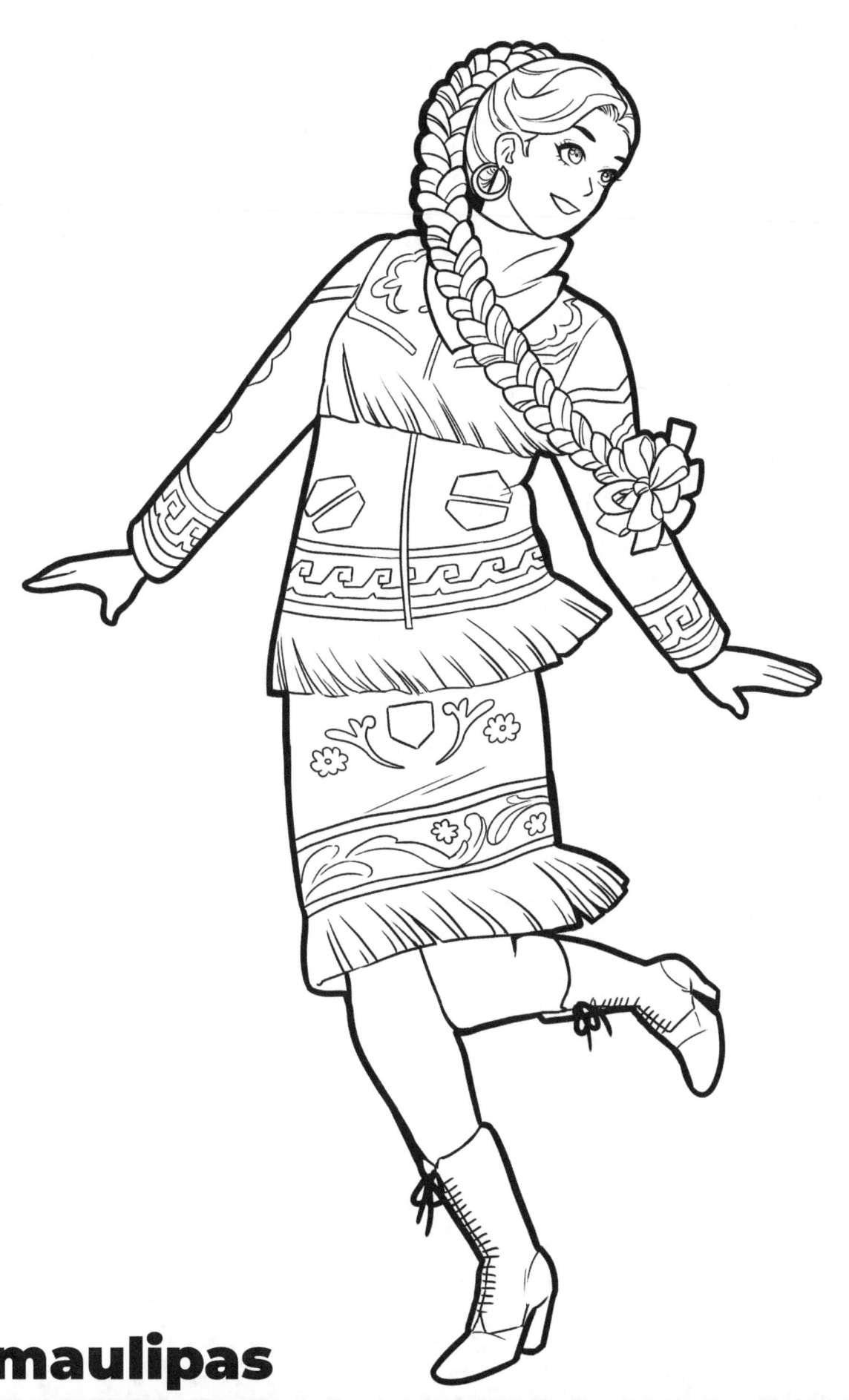

Tamaulipas

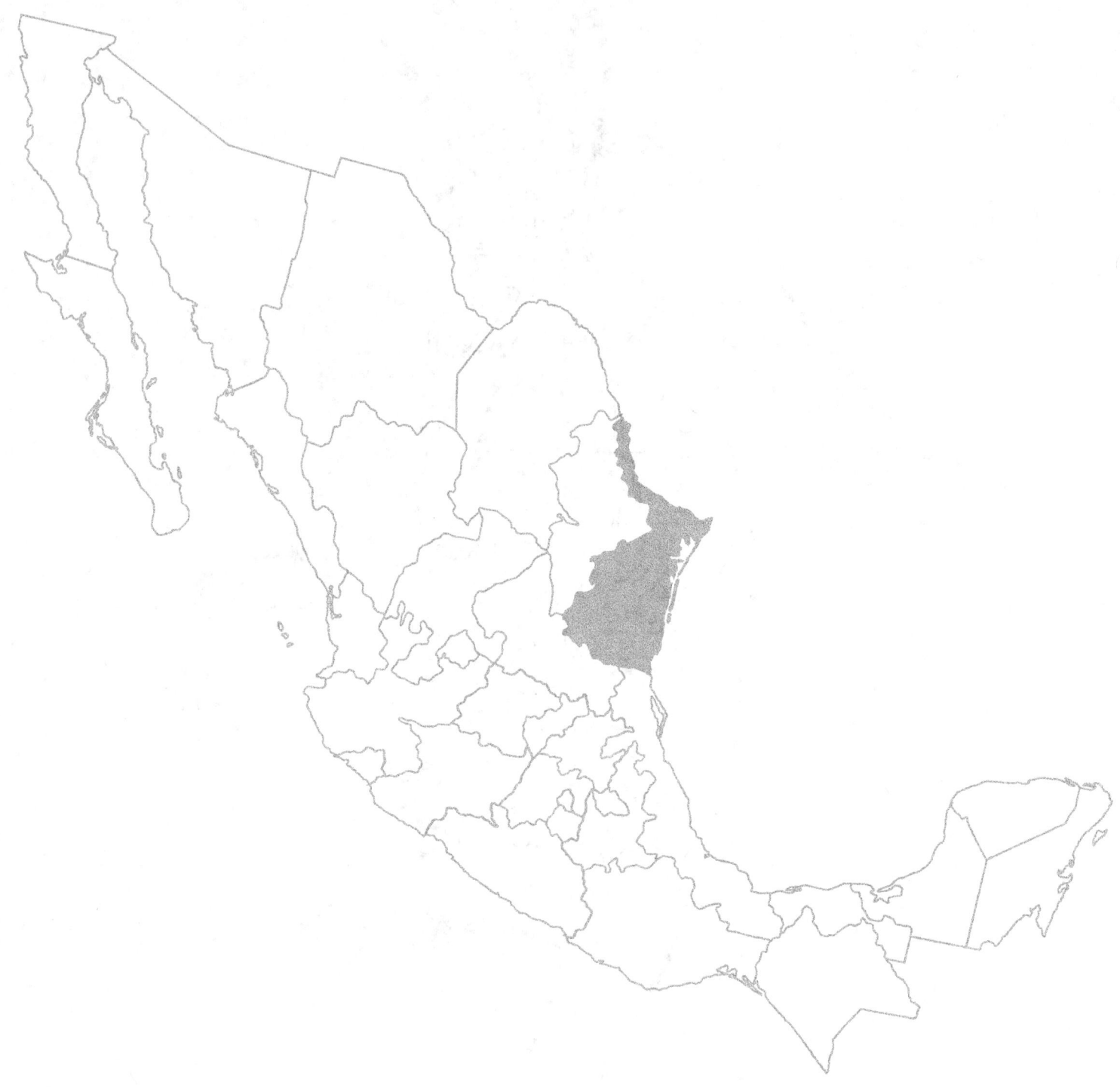

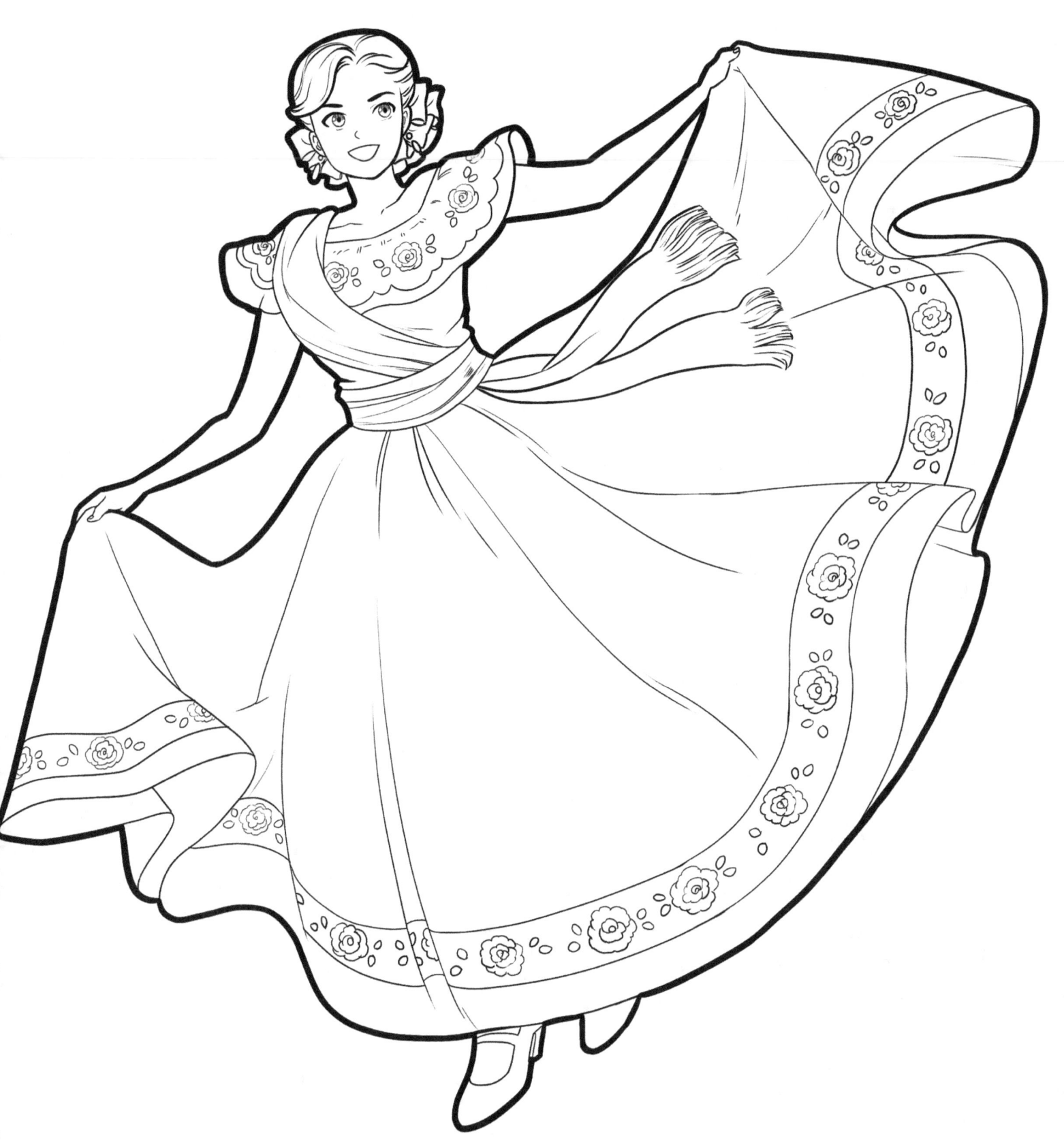

Zacatecas

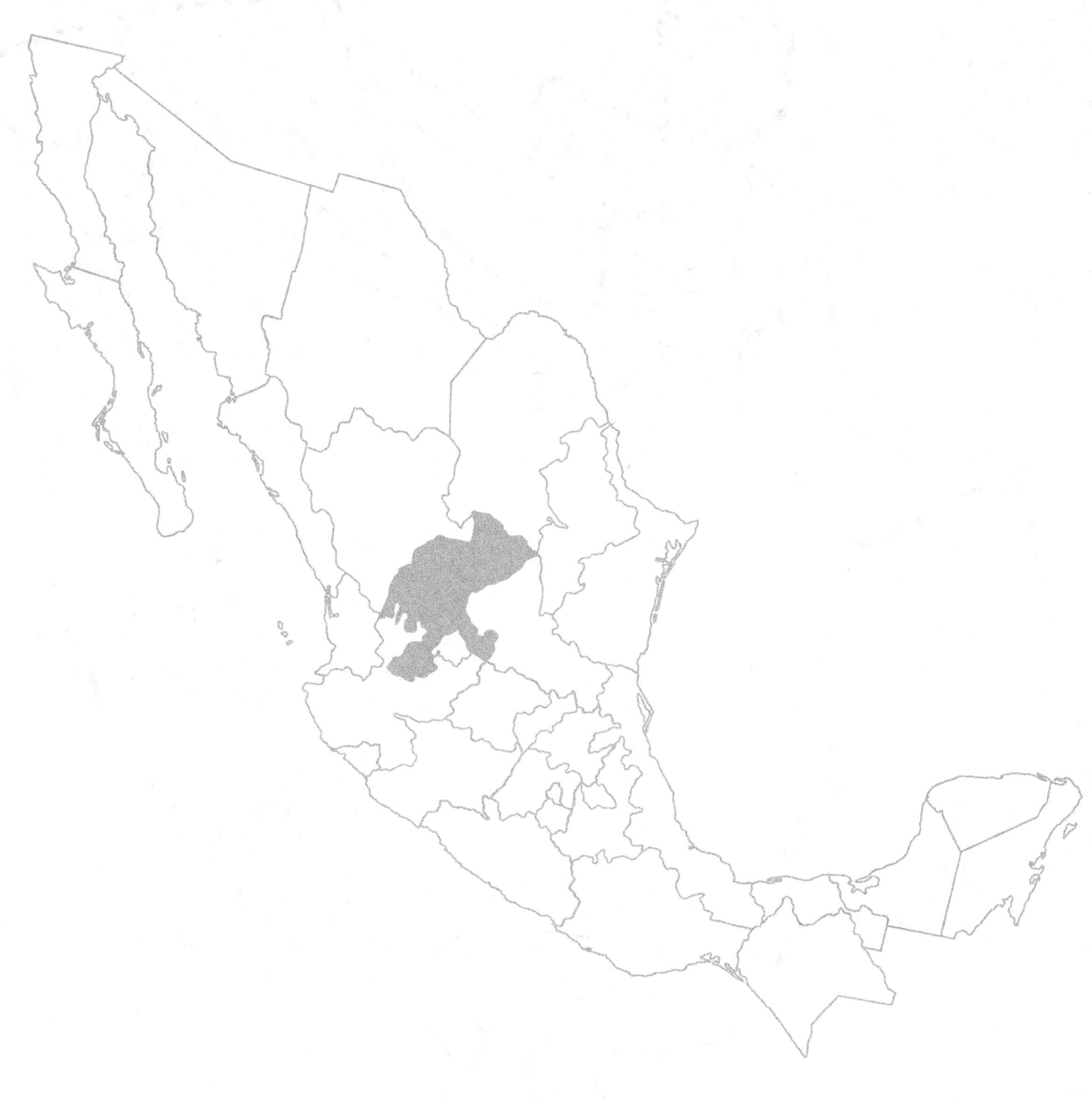

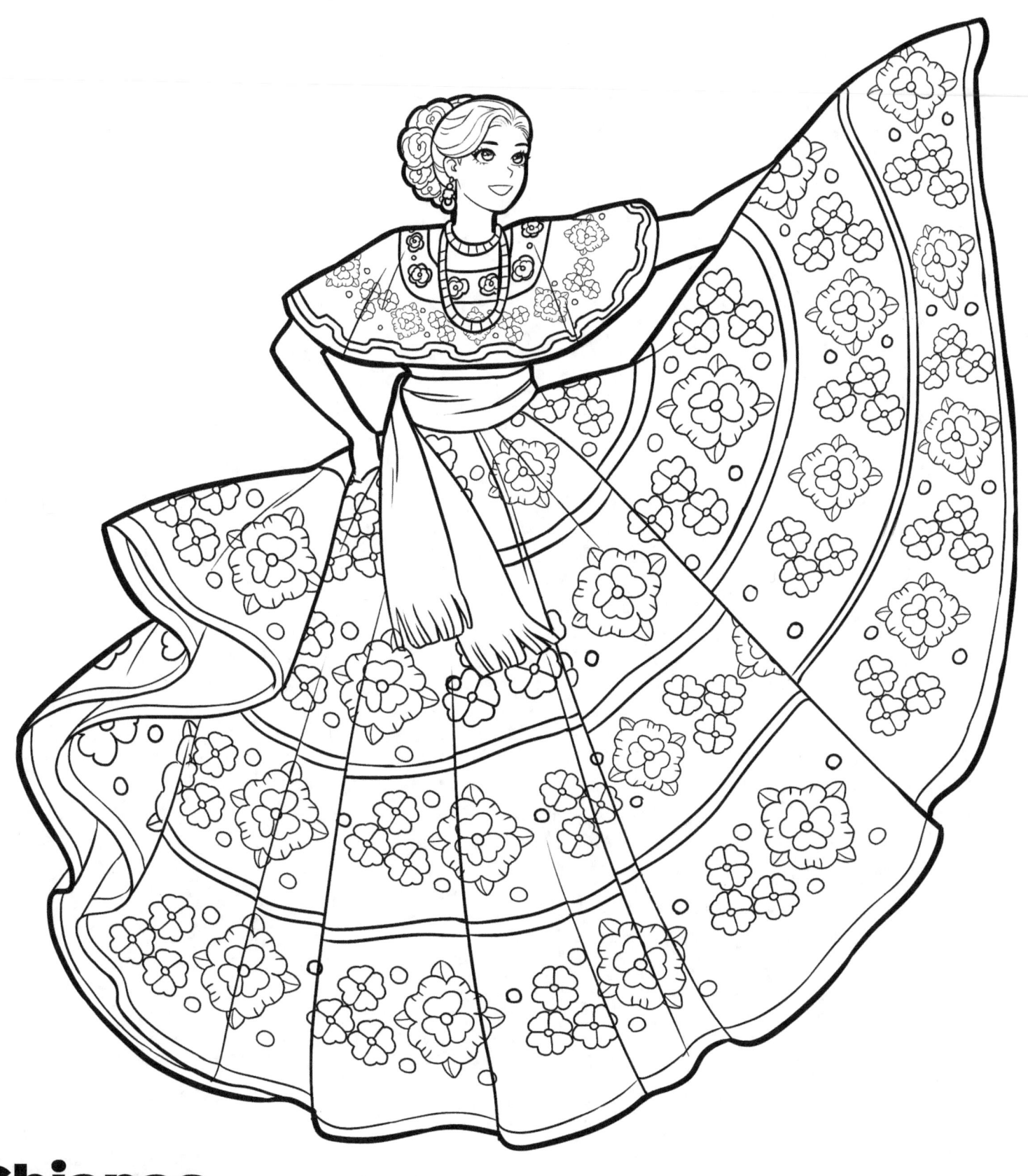

Chiapas

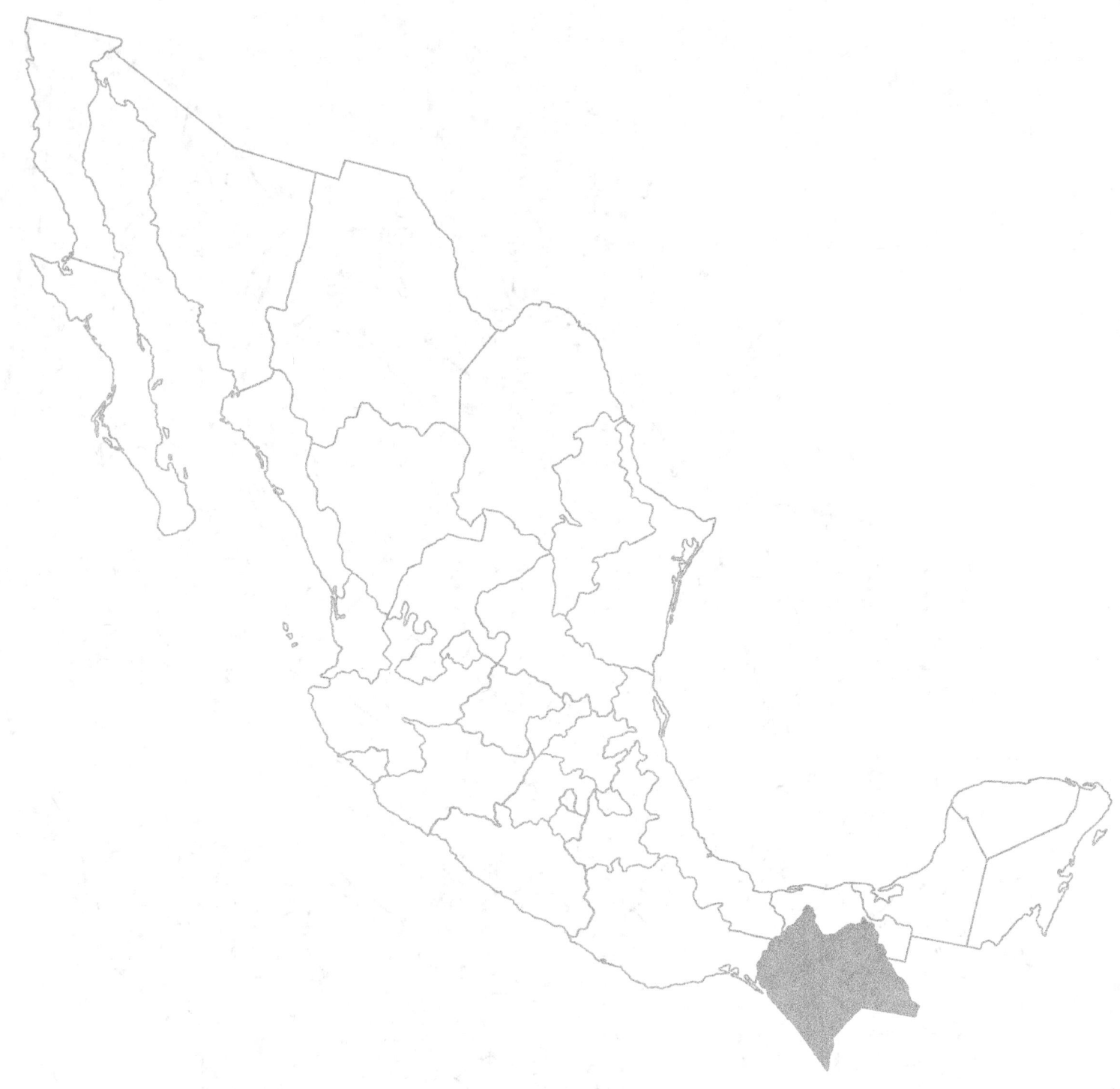

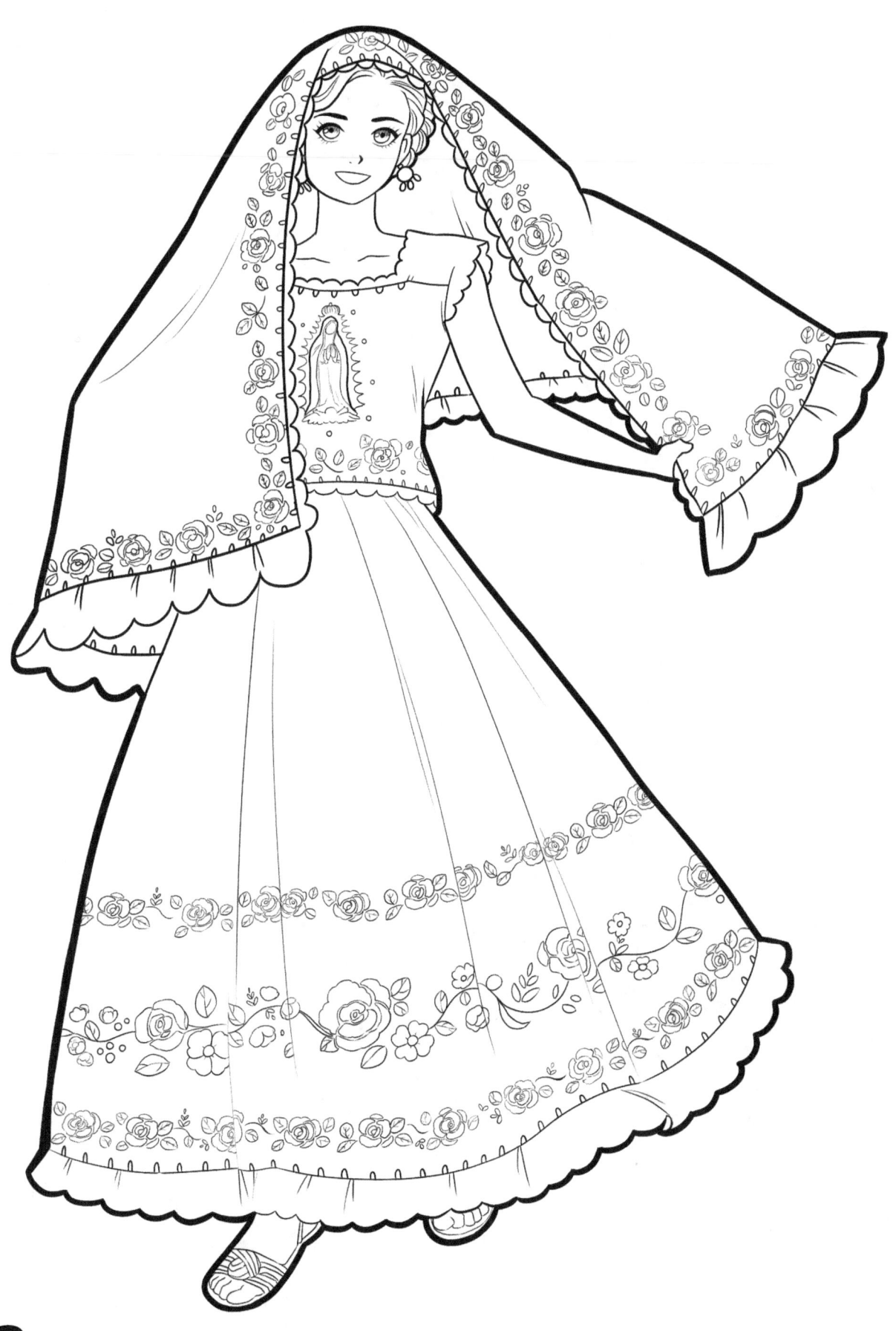

Colima

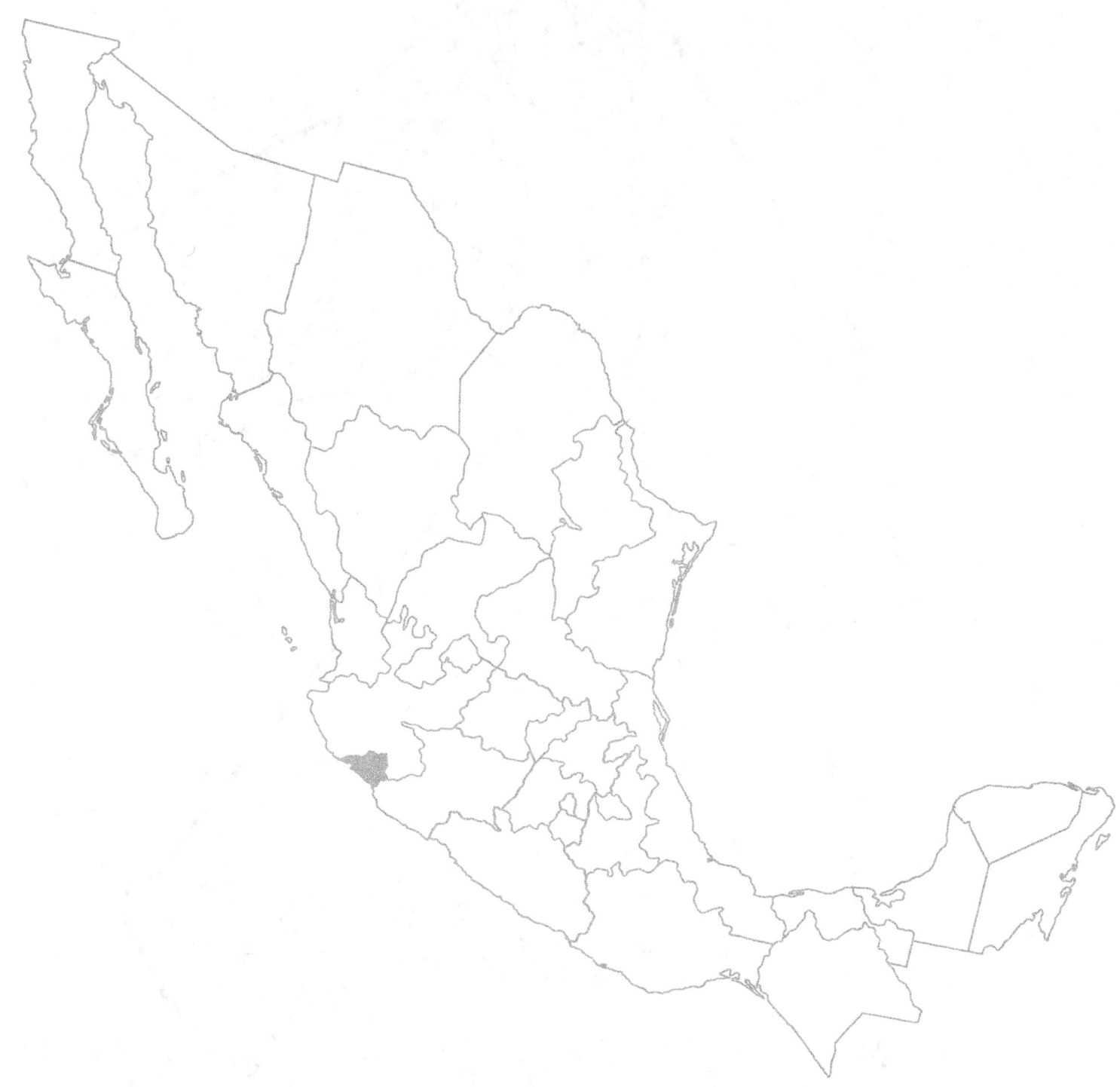

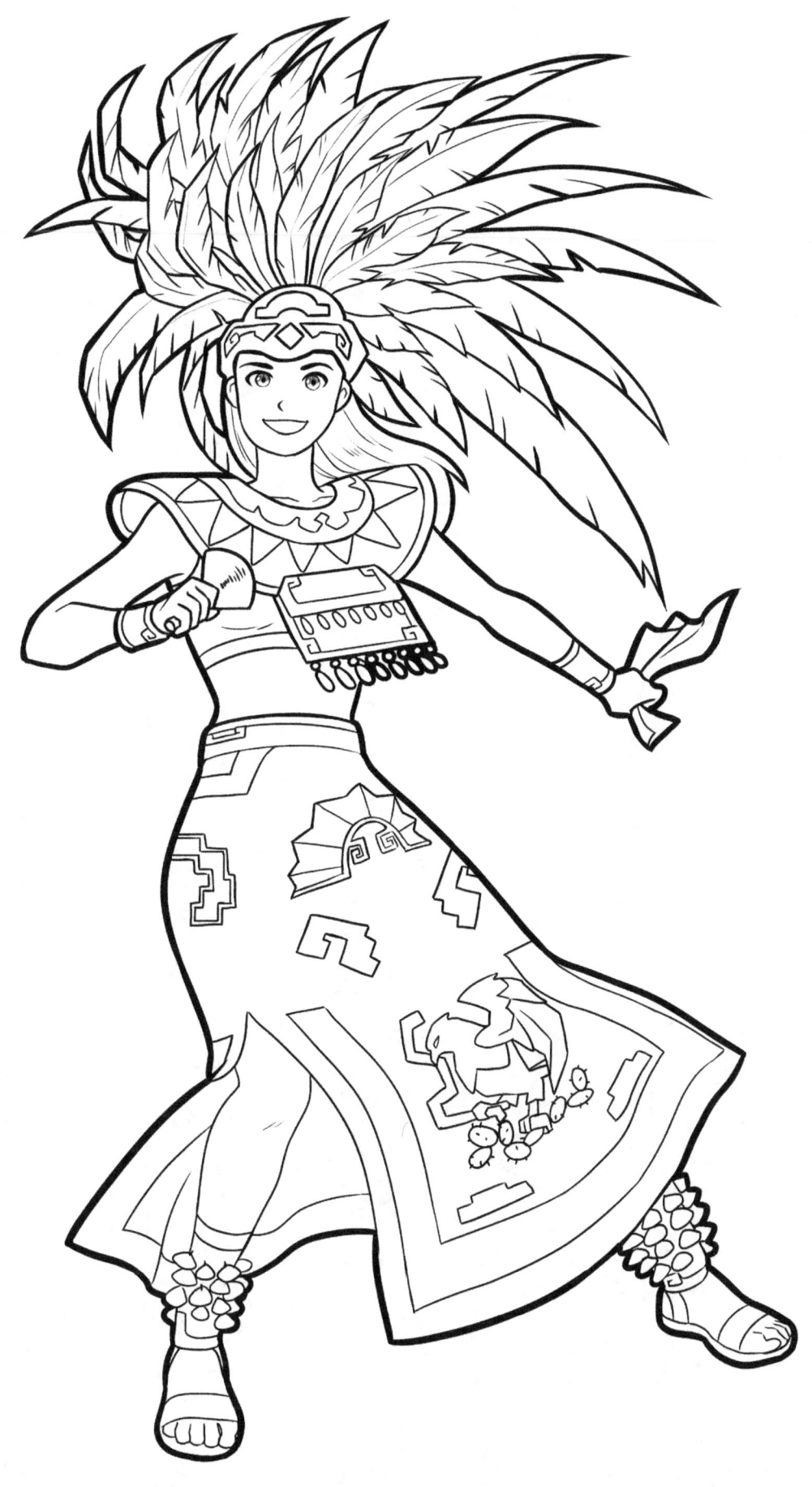

Distrito Federal (D.F.) - Azteca

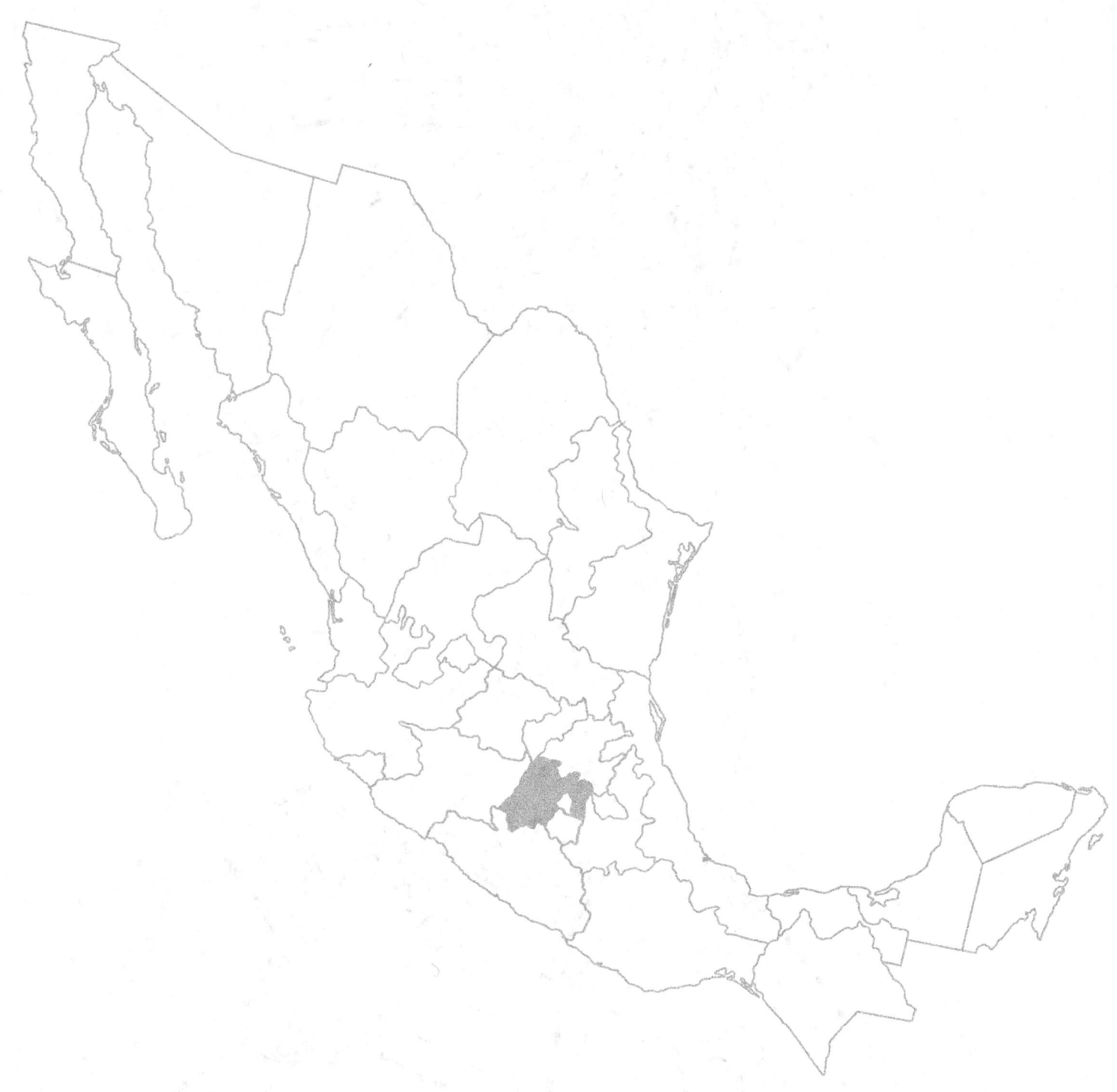

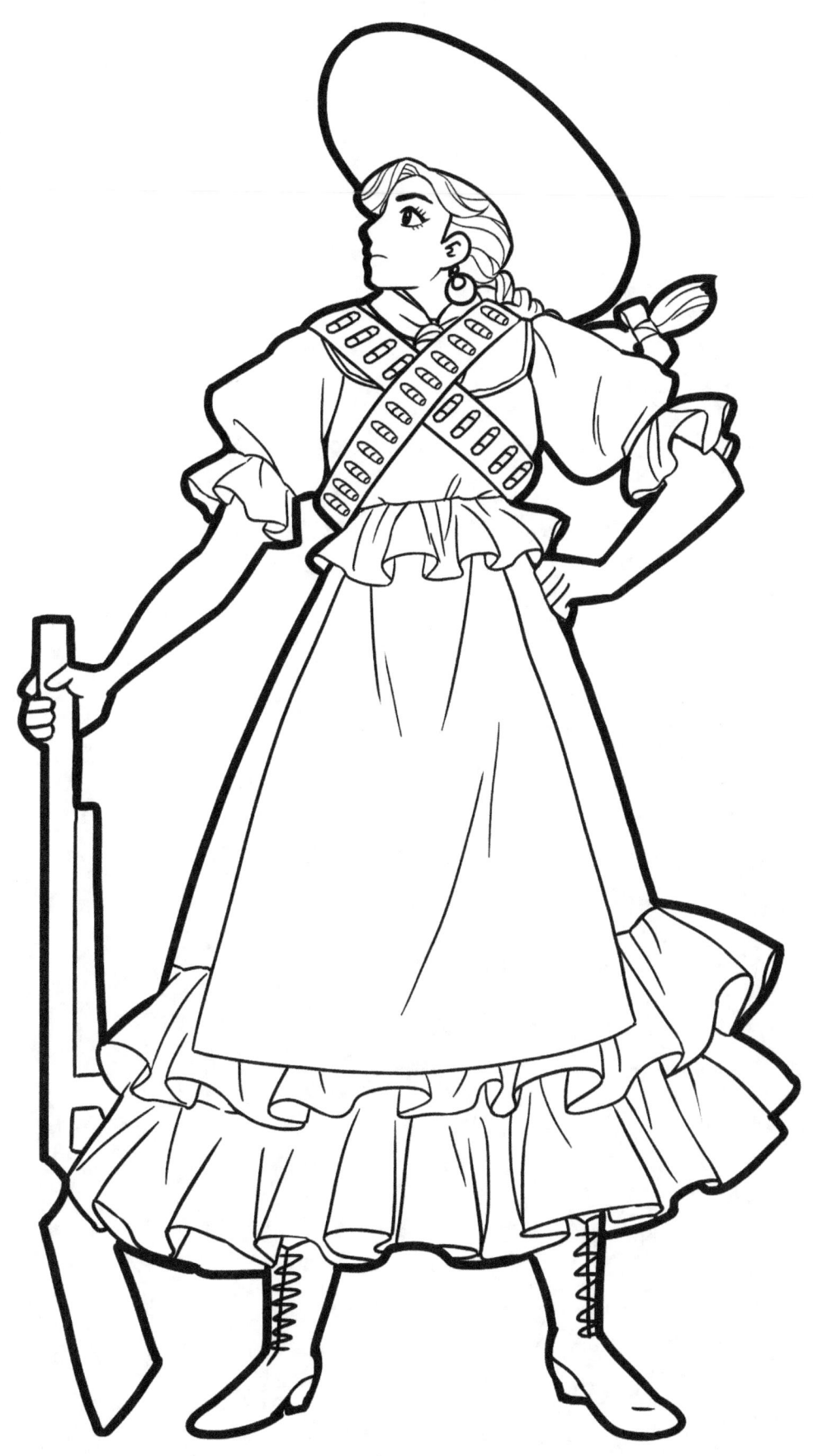

Soldaderas de la Revolución de 1910

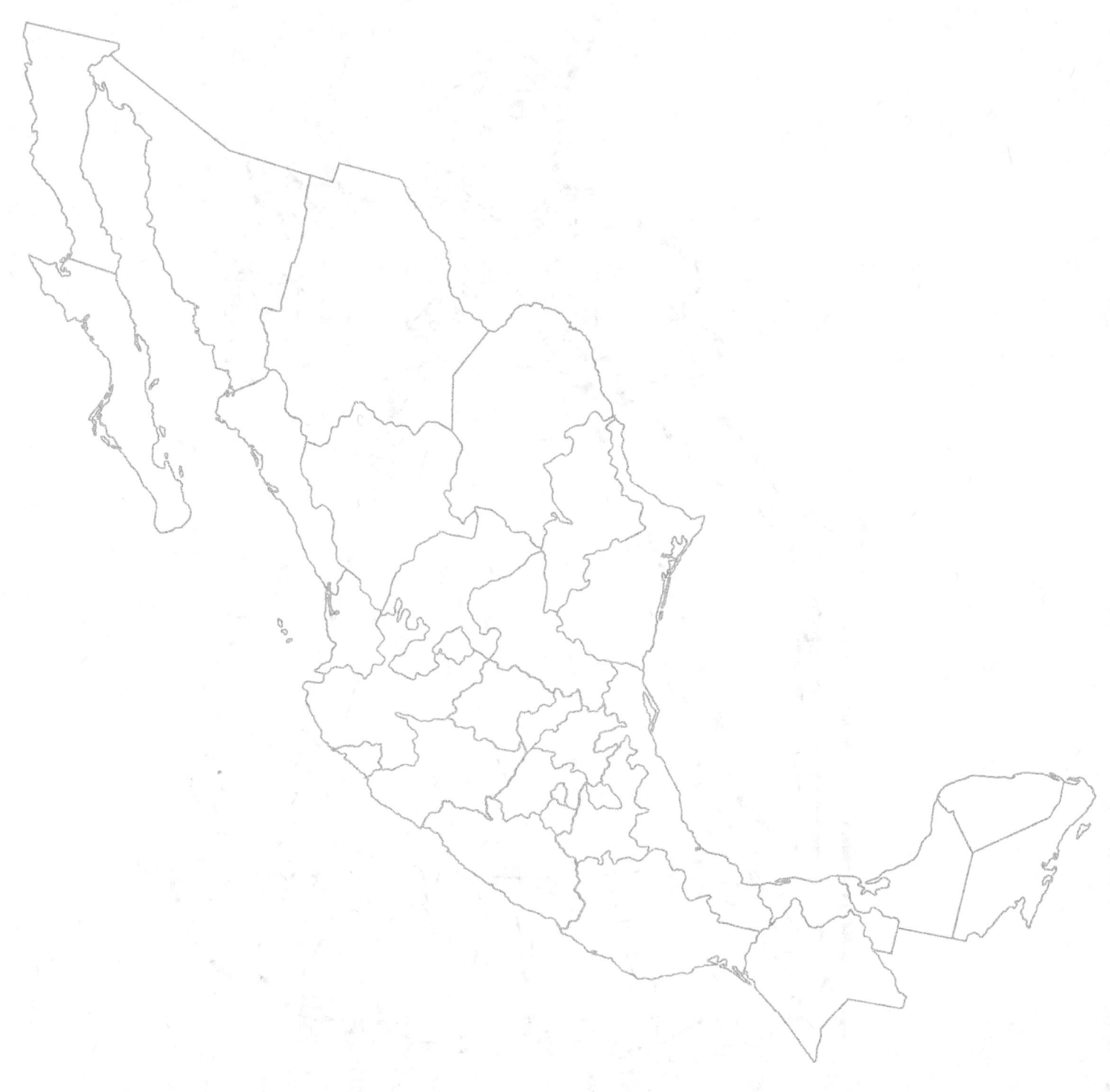

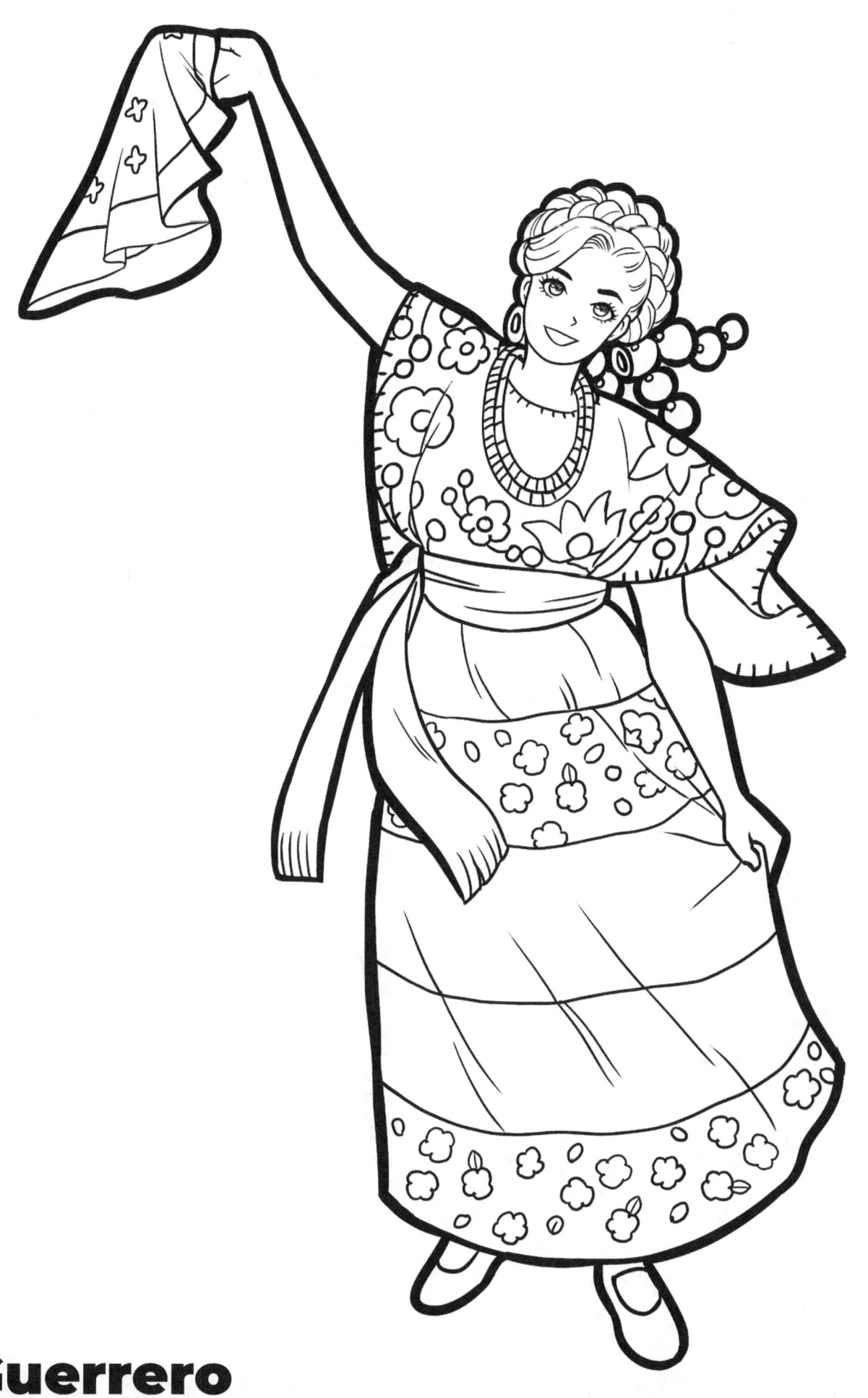

Guerrero

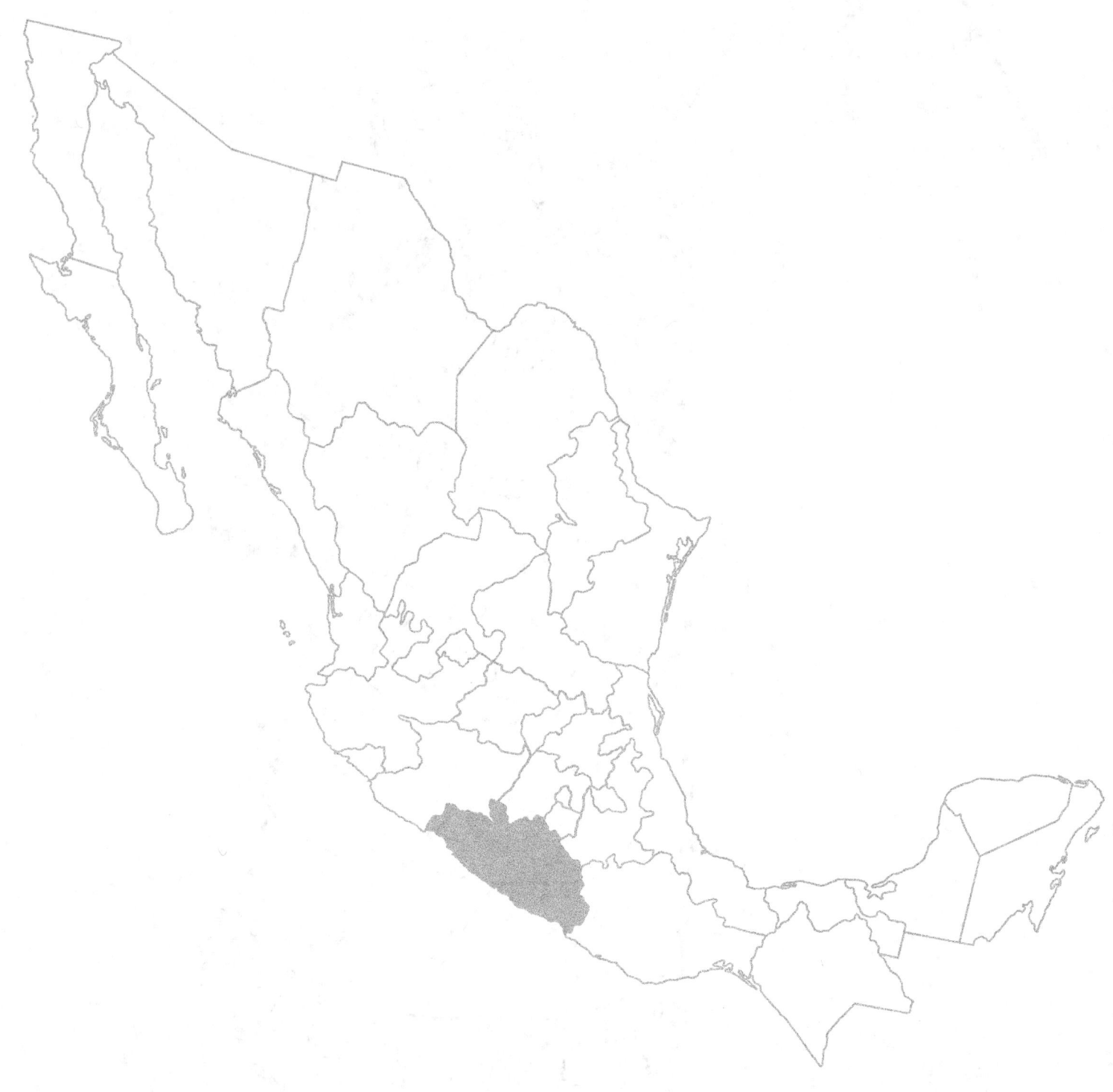

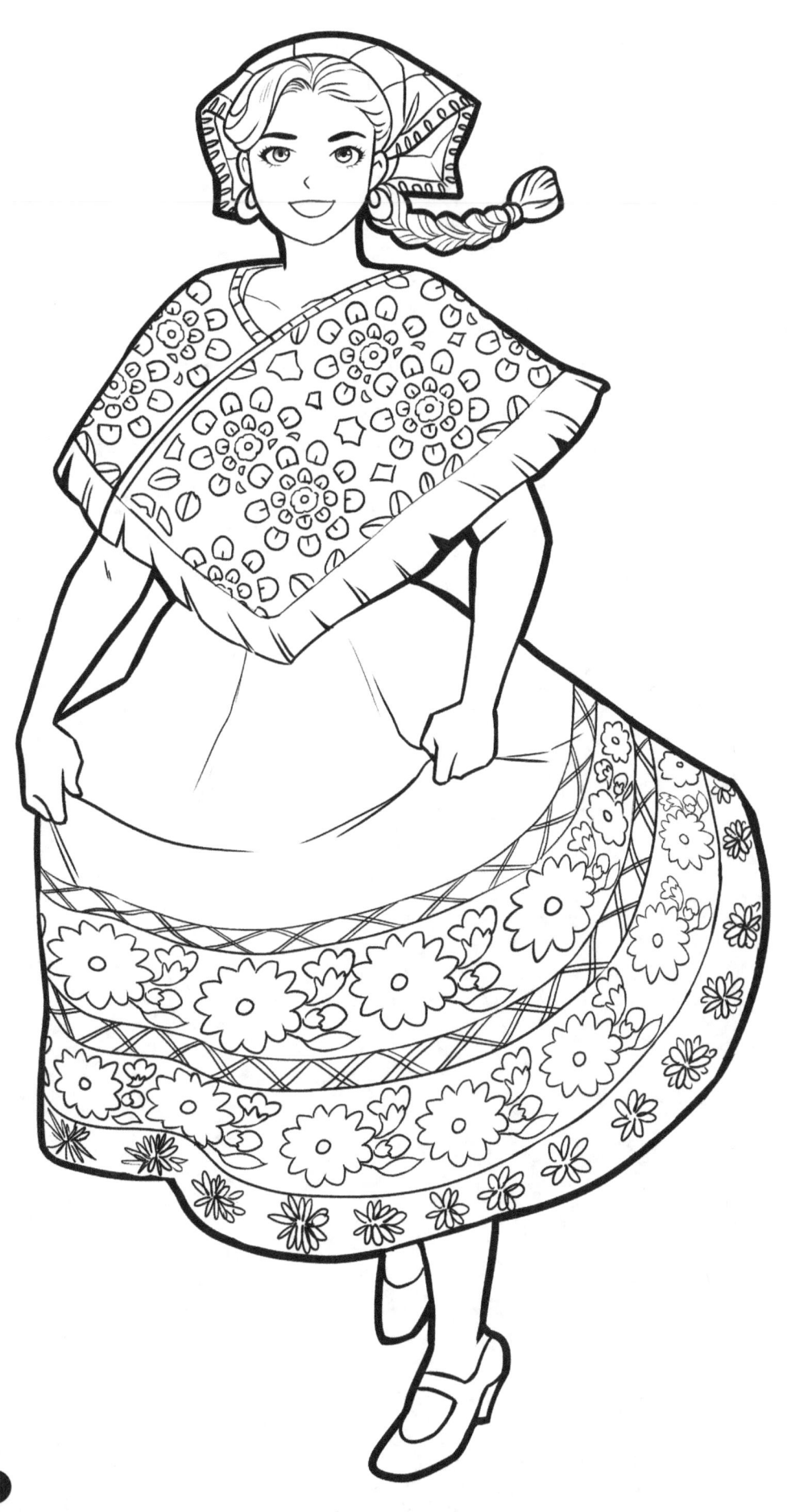

Hidalgo

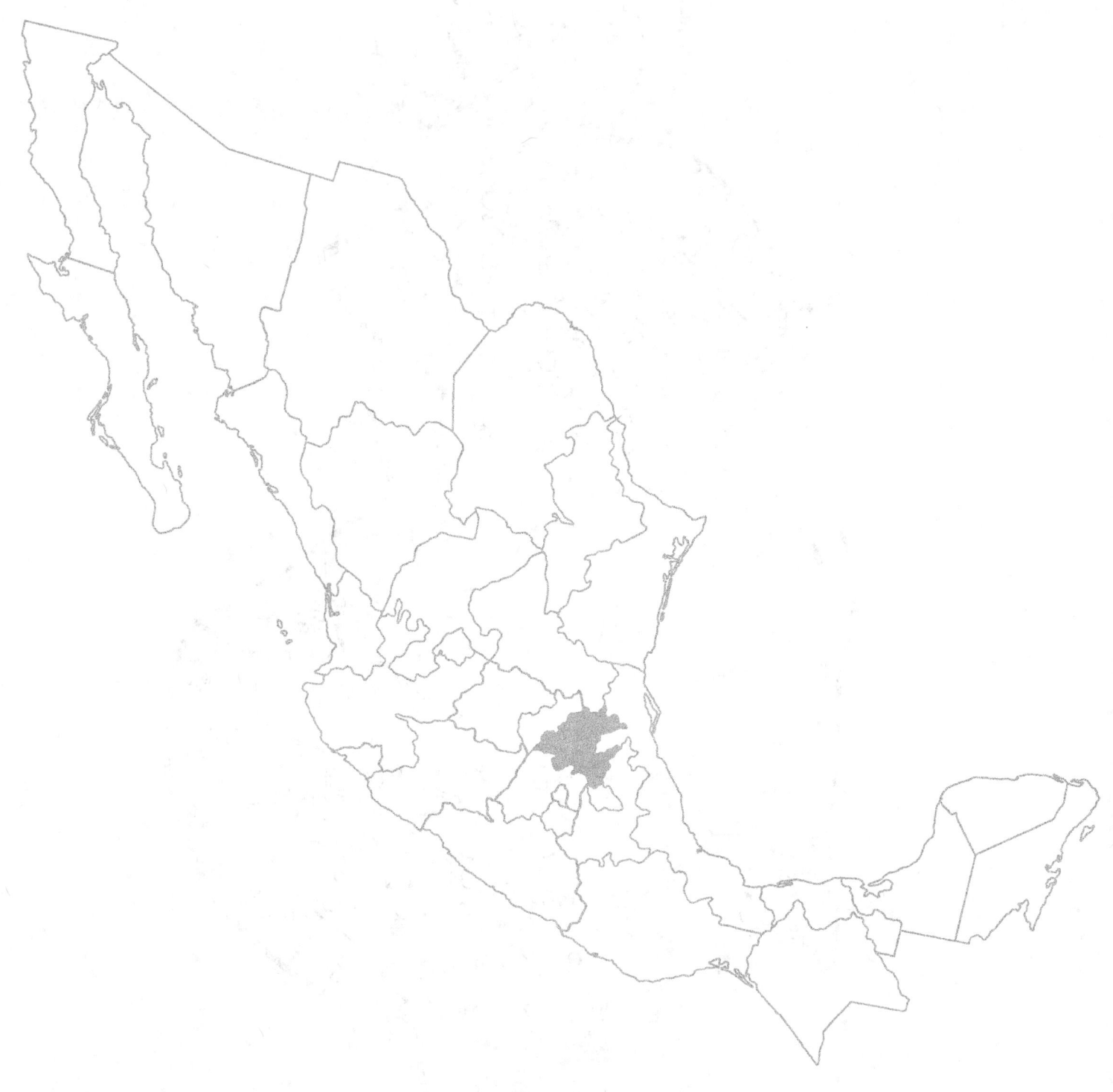

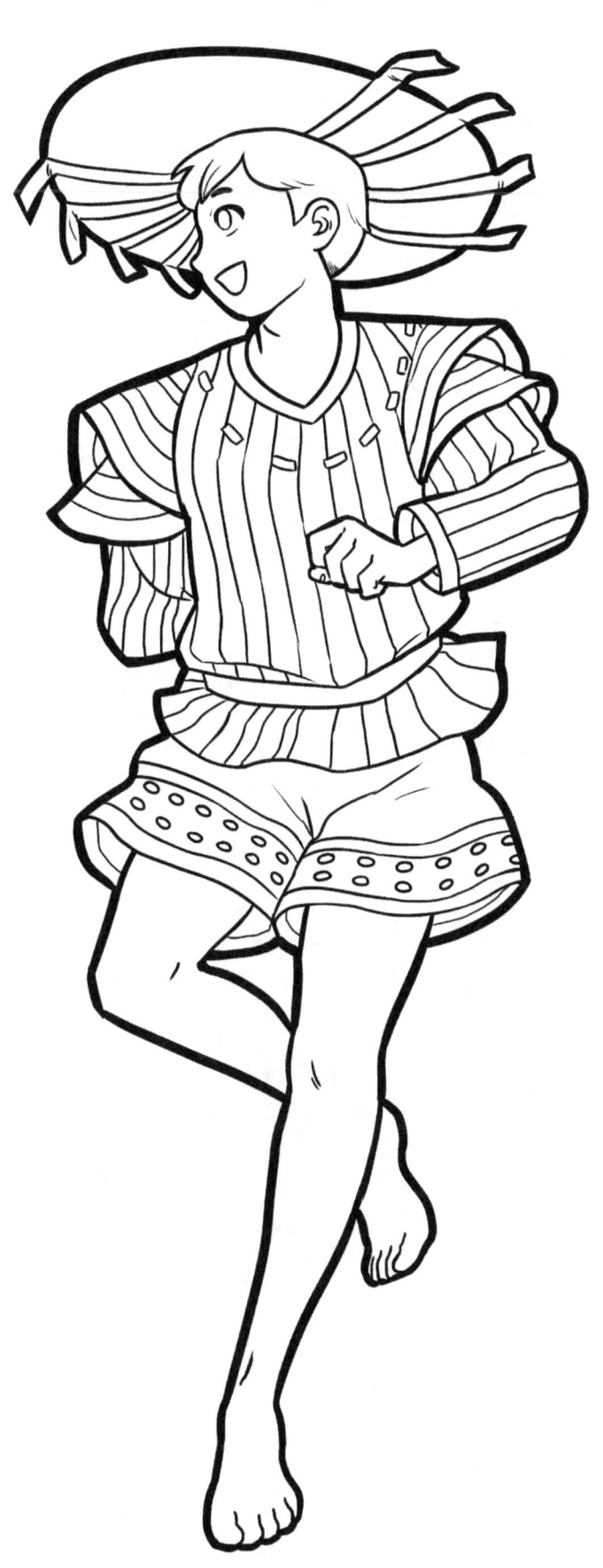

Mixteco

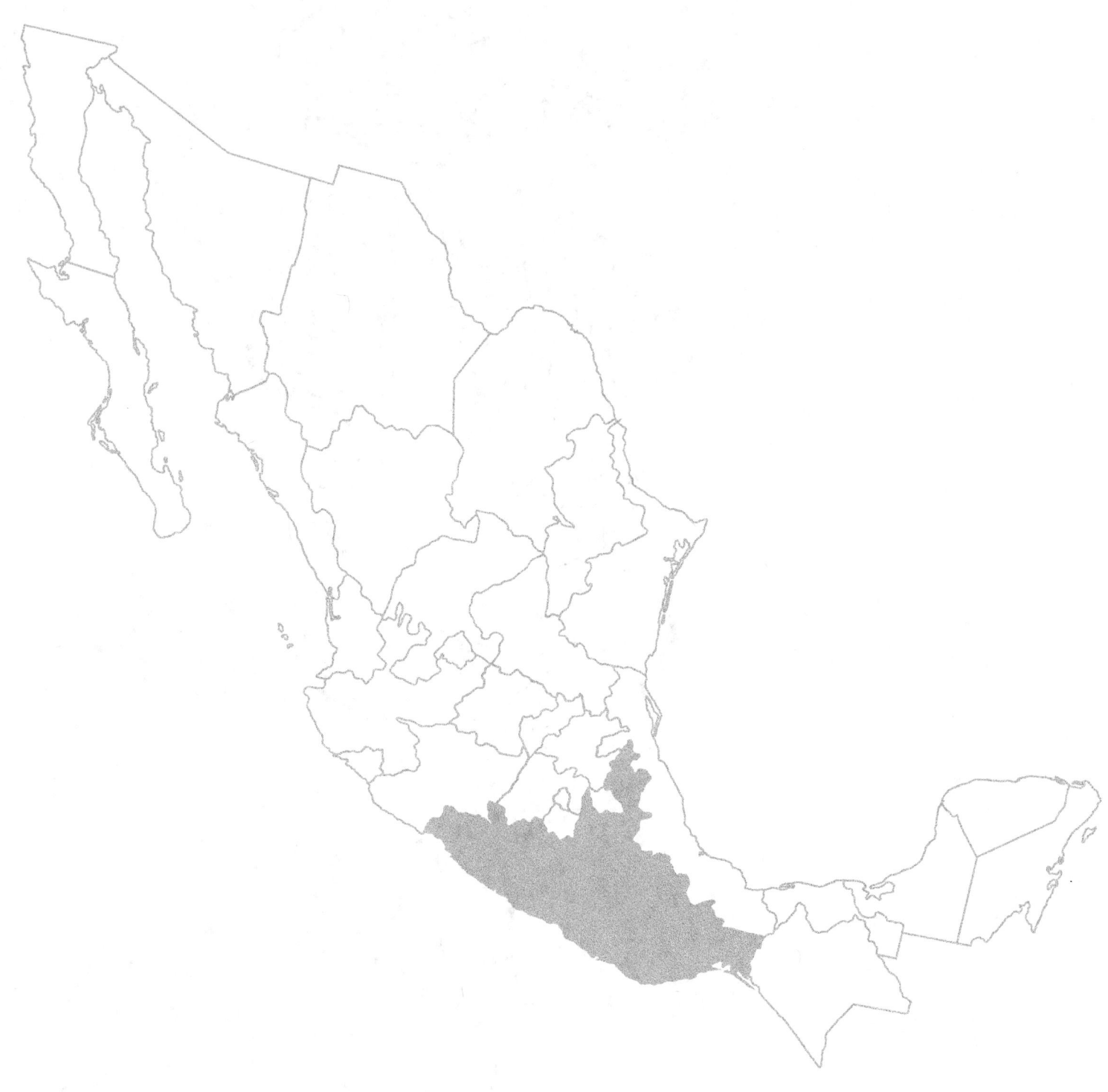

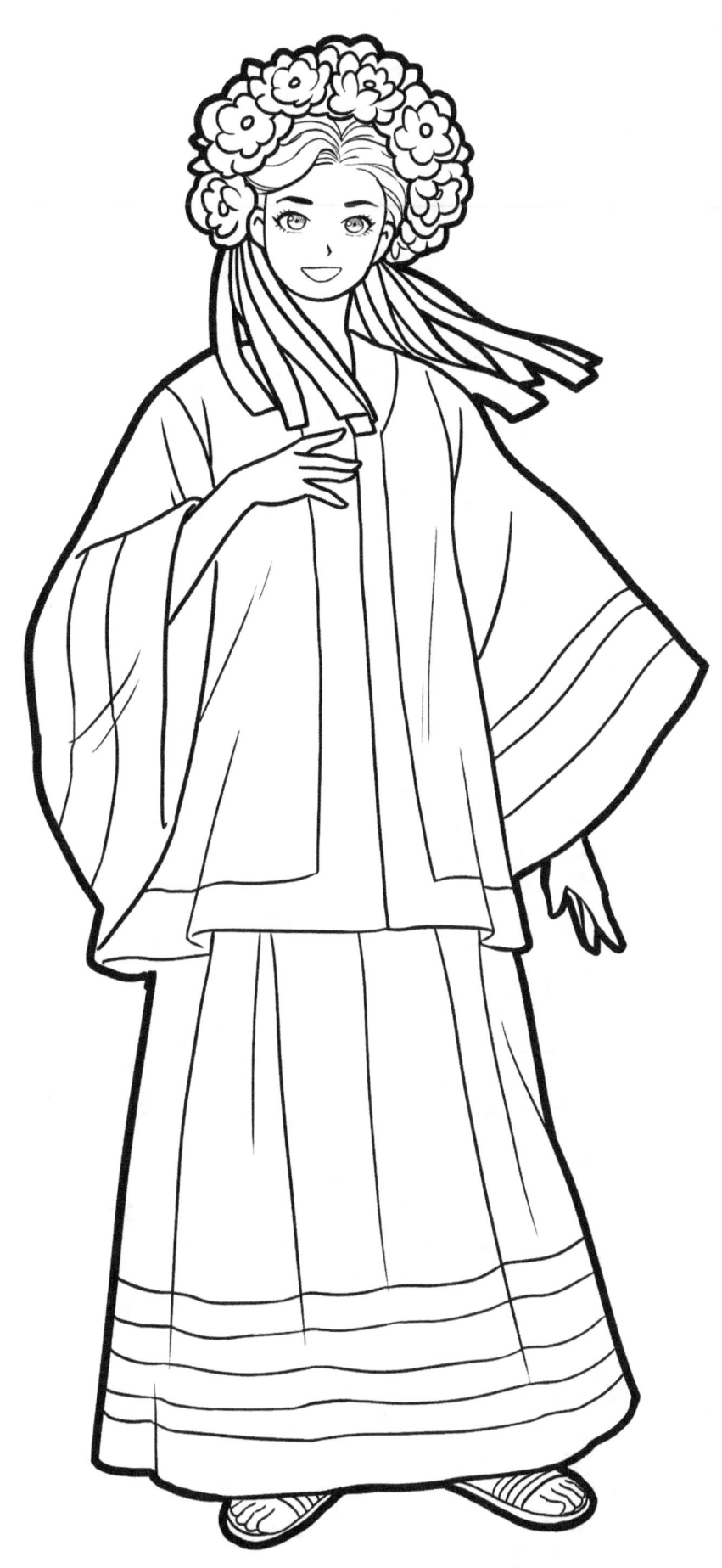

Morelos

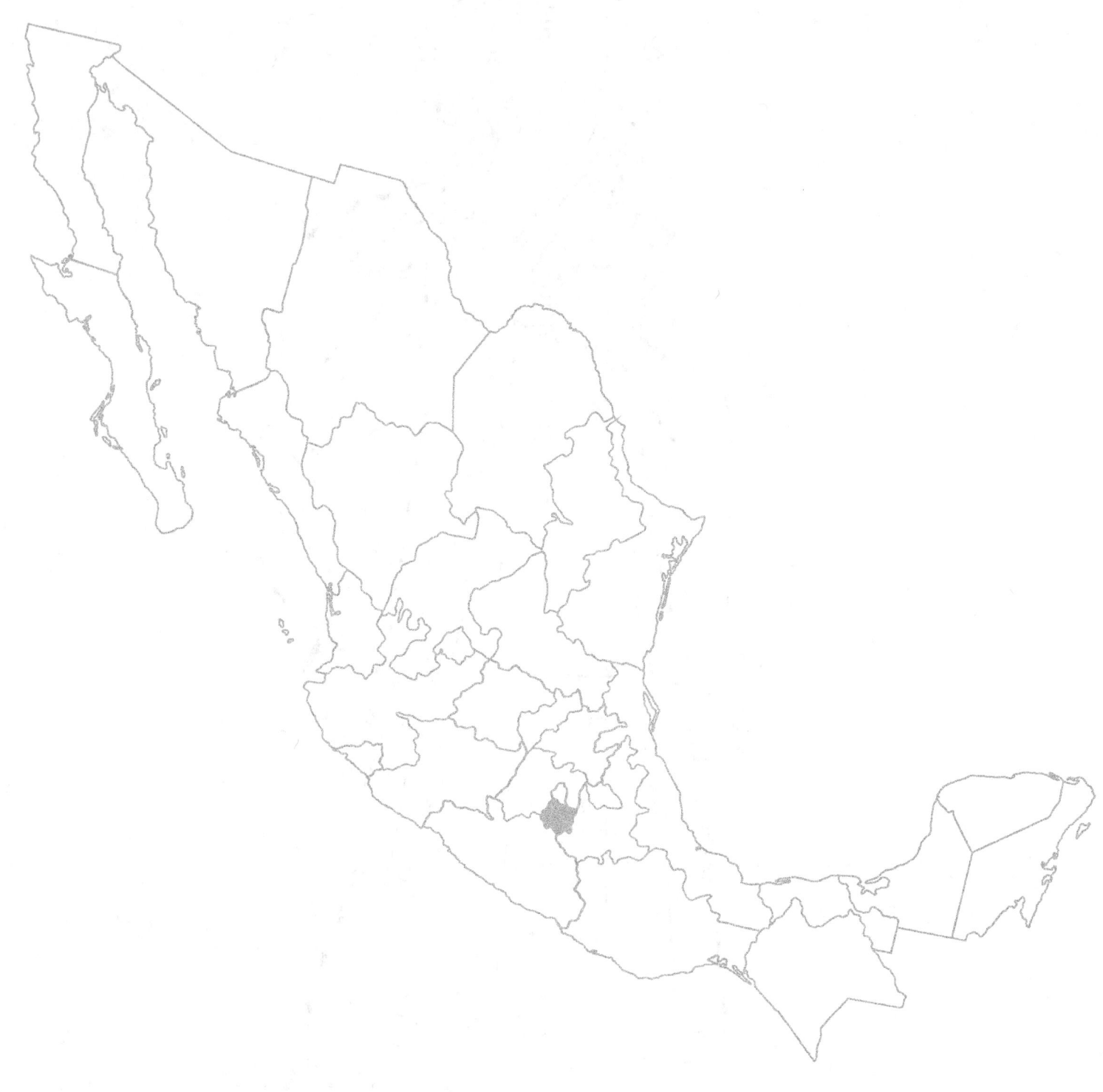

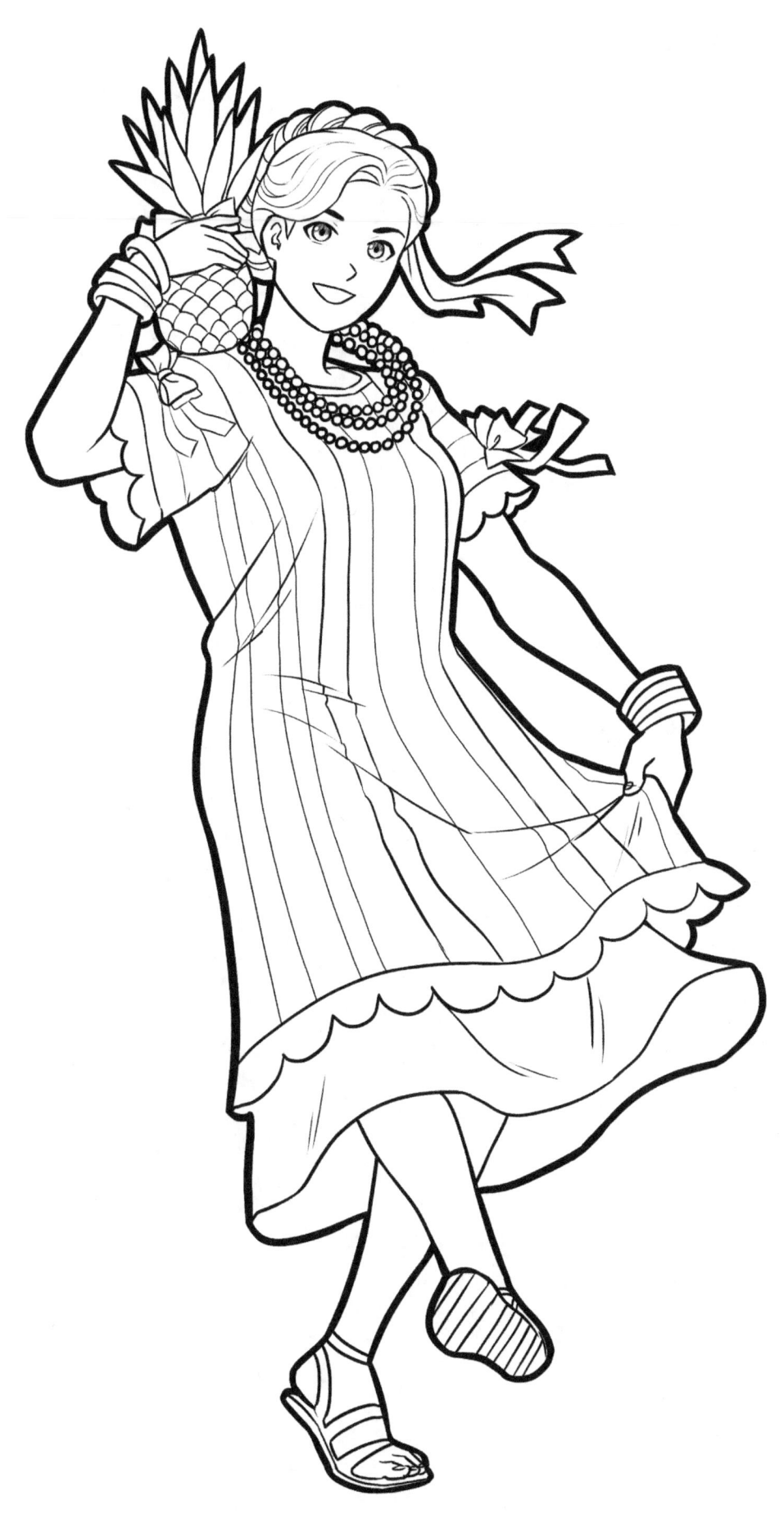

Oaxaca

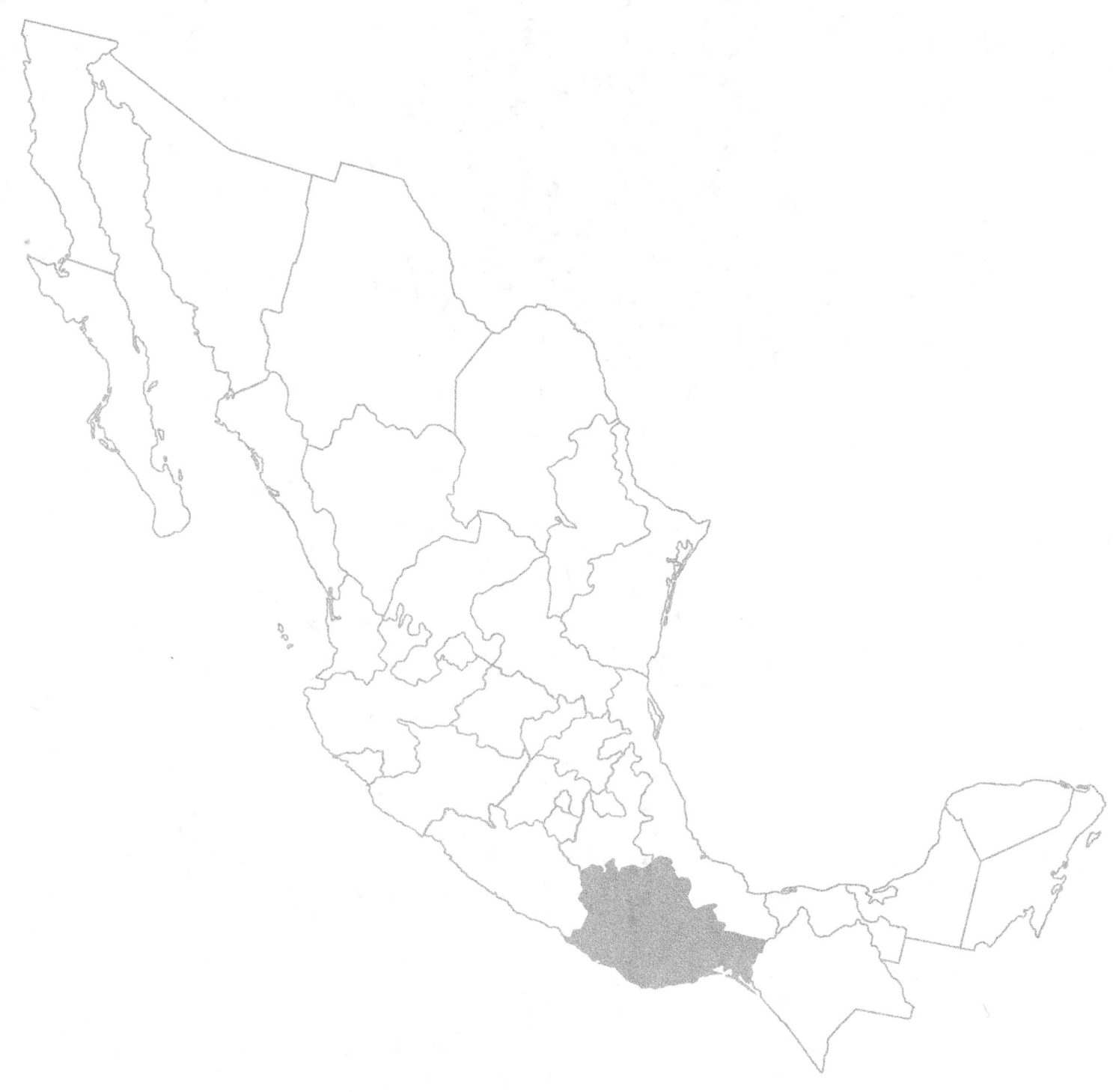

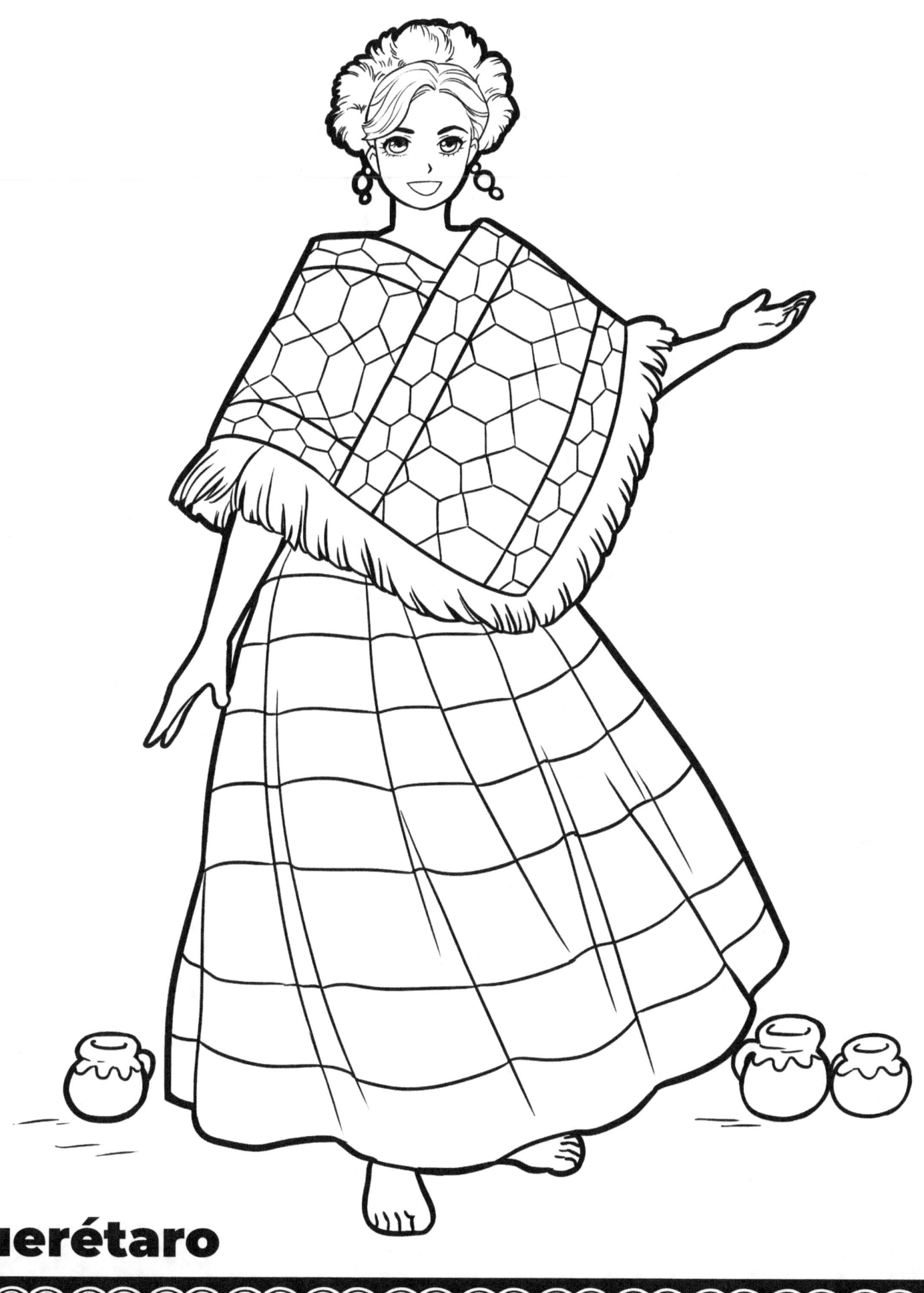

Querétaro

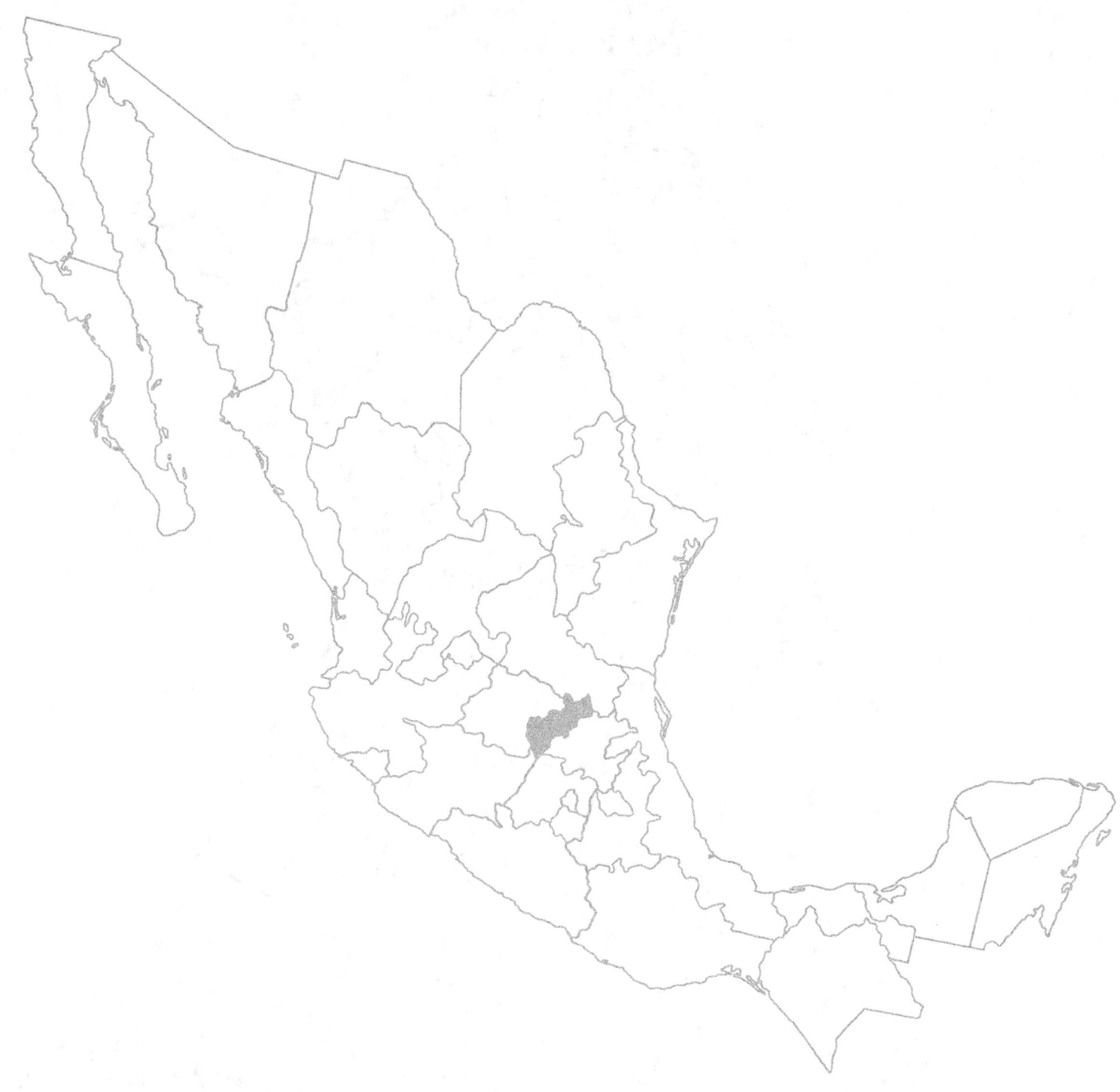

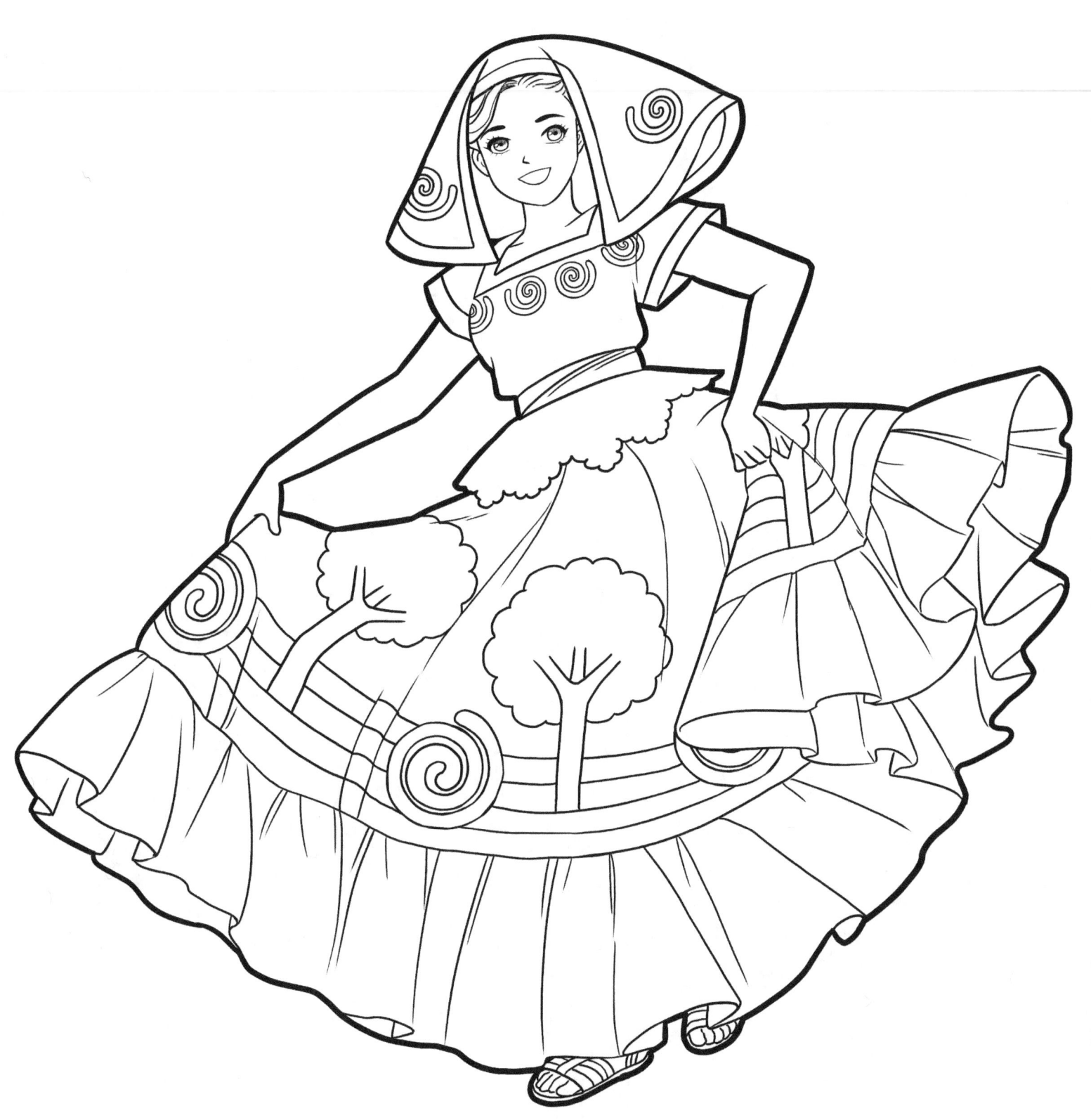

Quintana Roo

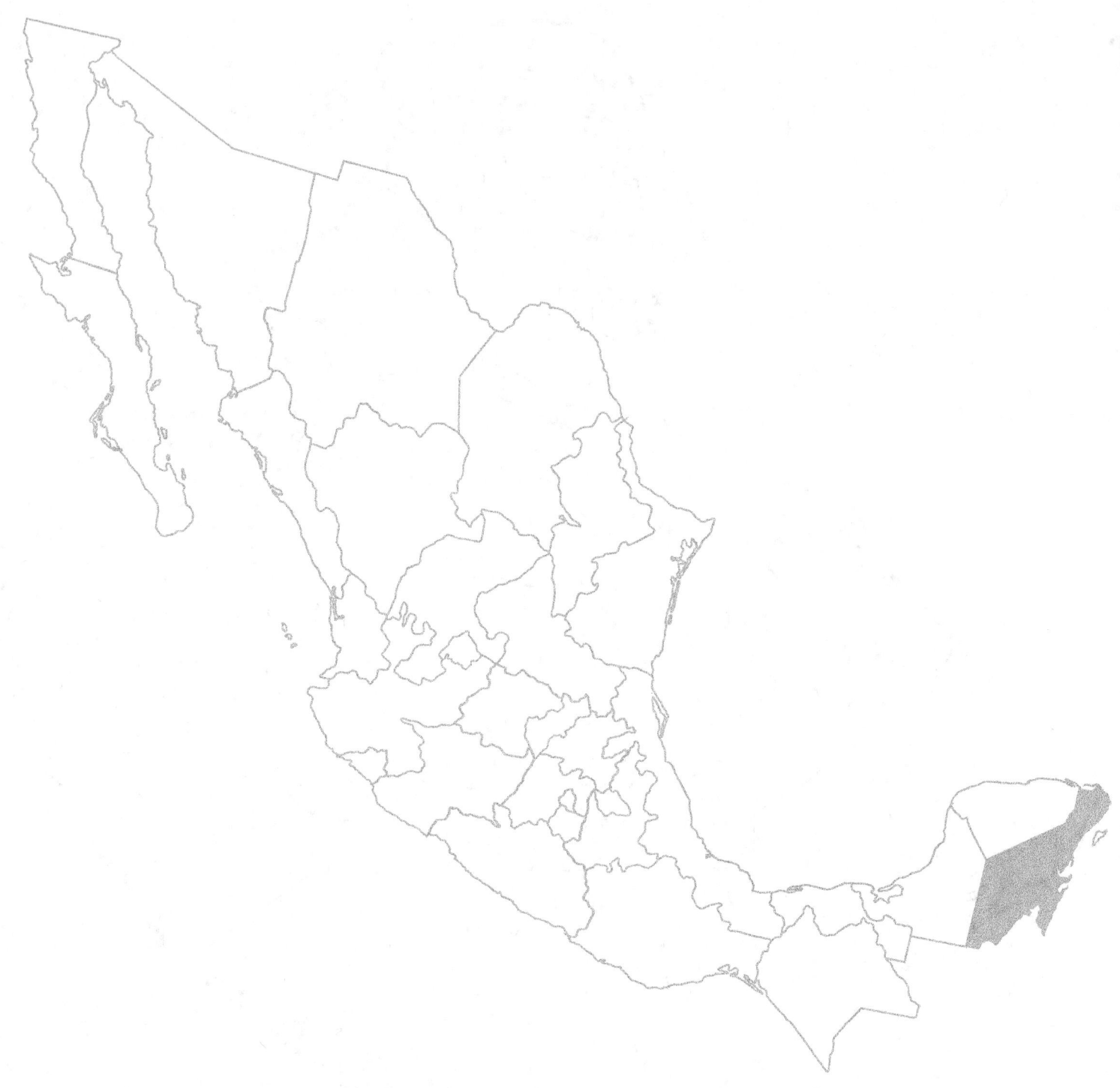

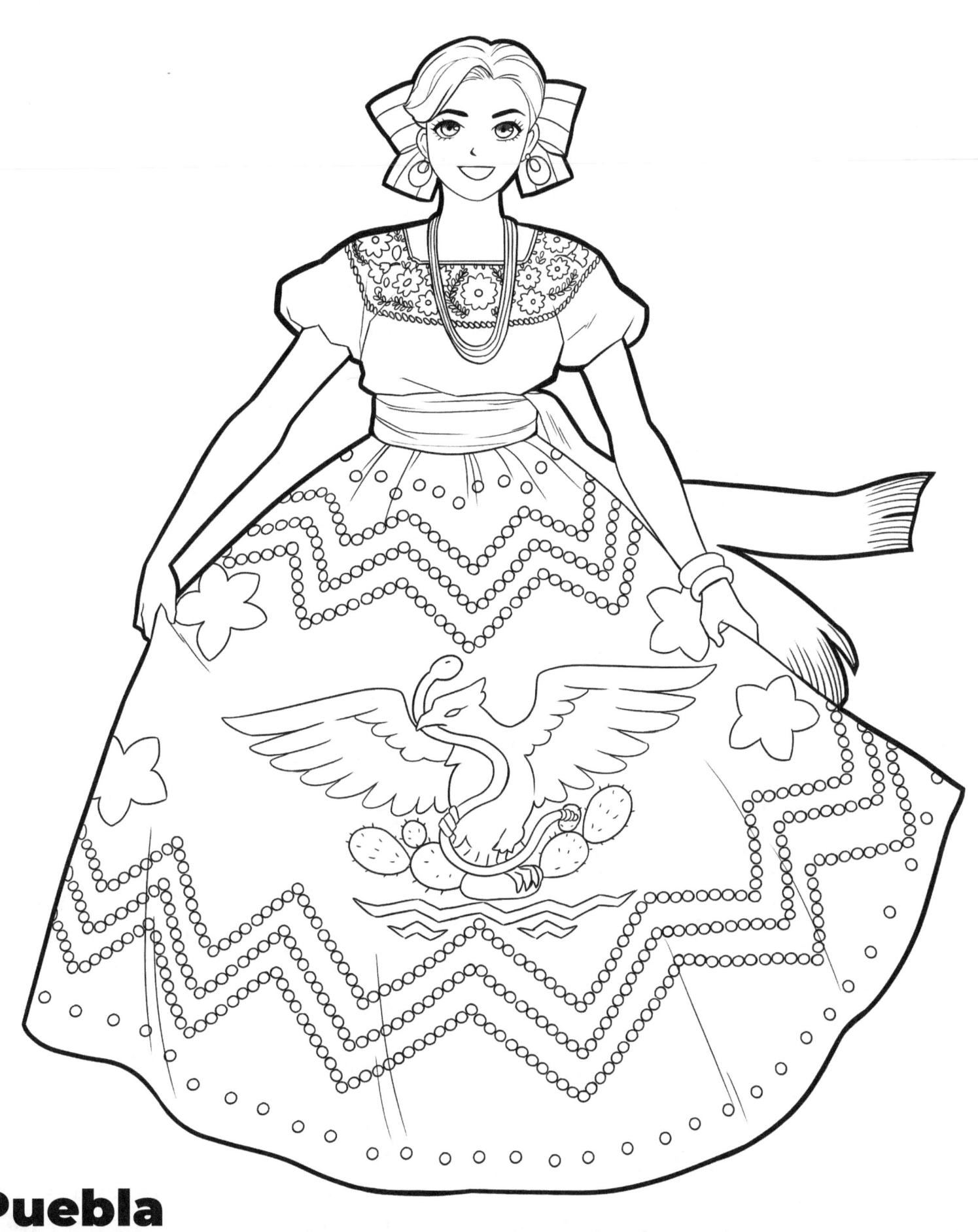

Puebla

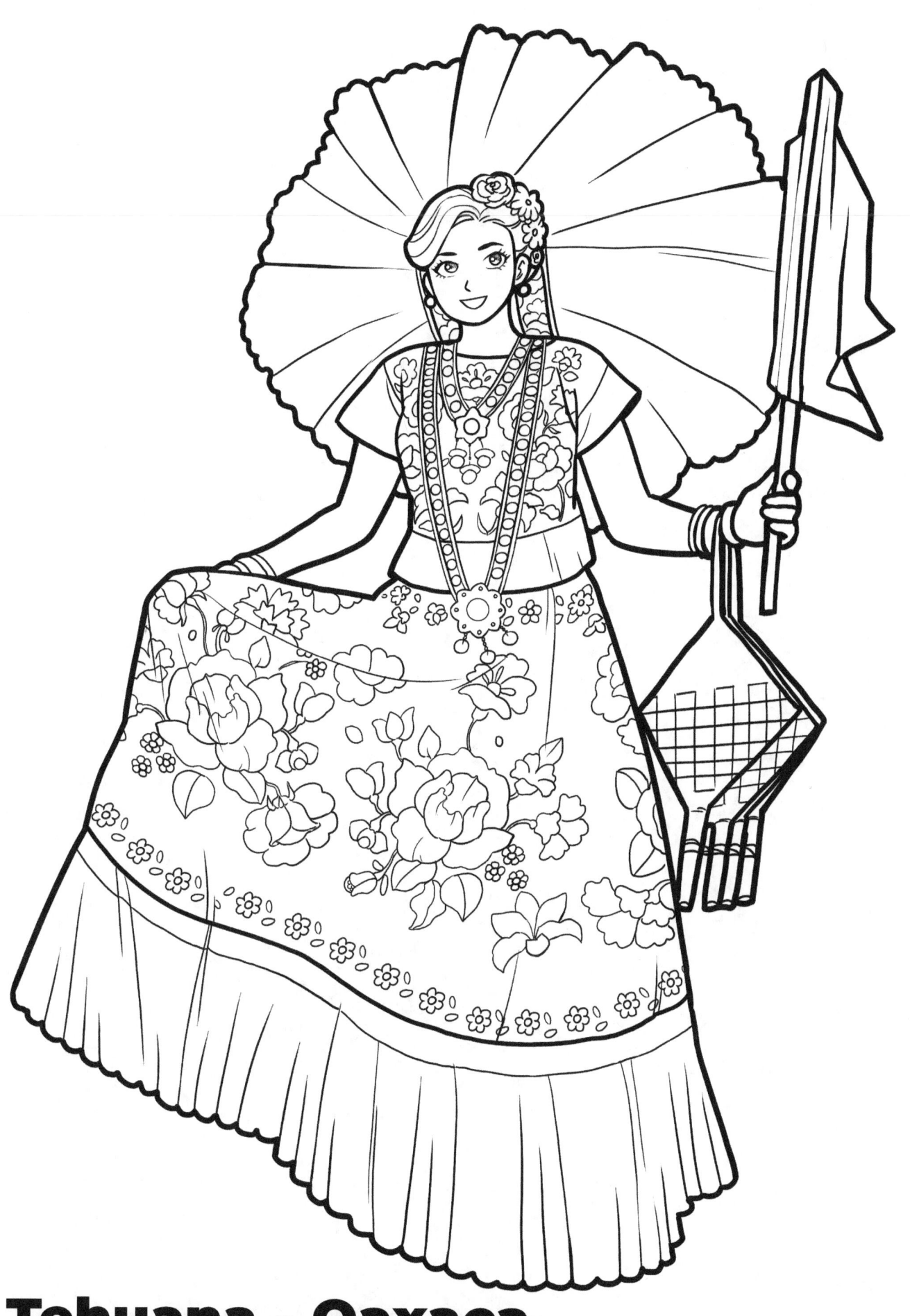

La Tehuana - Oaxaca

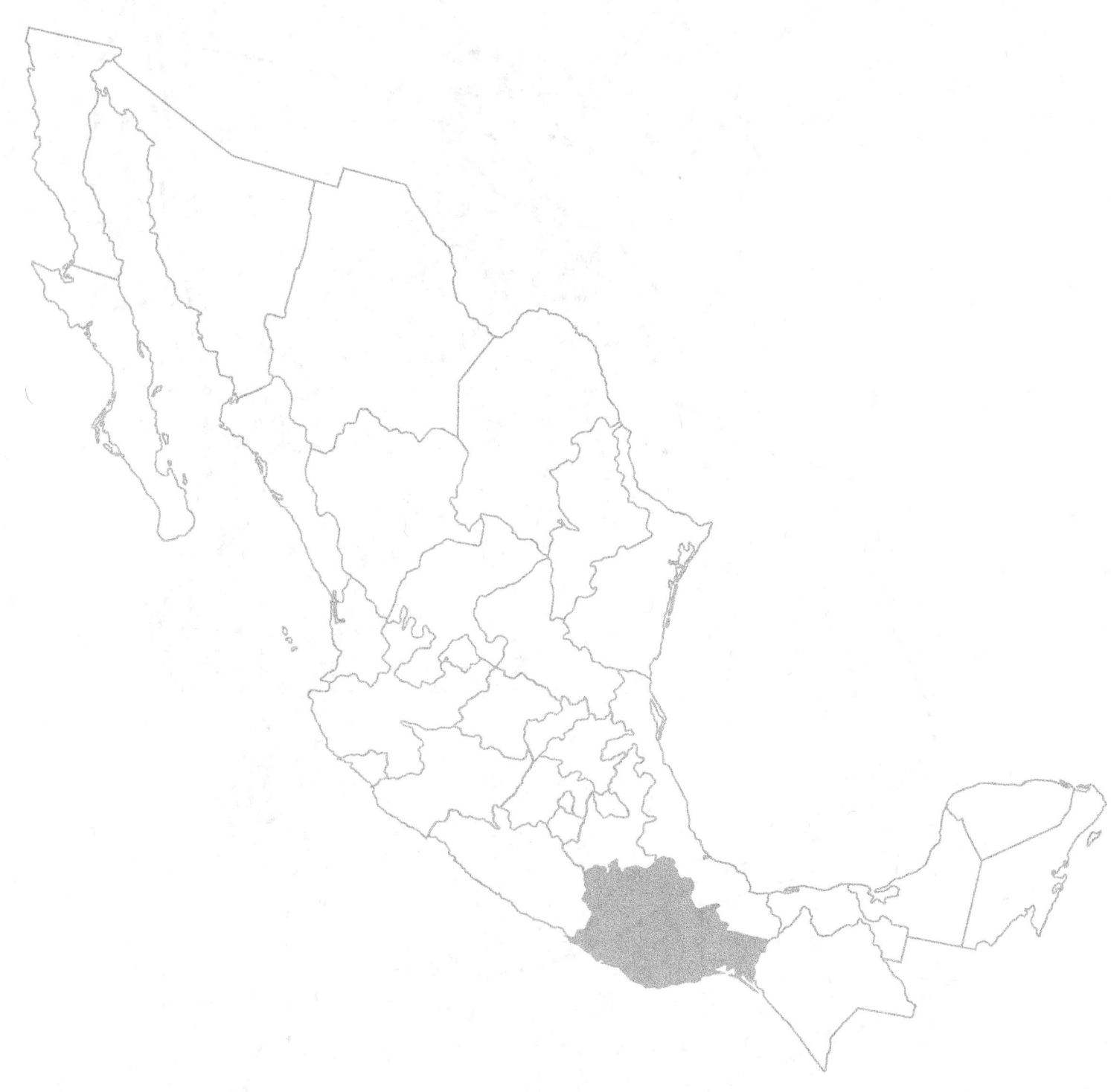

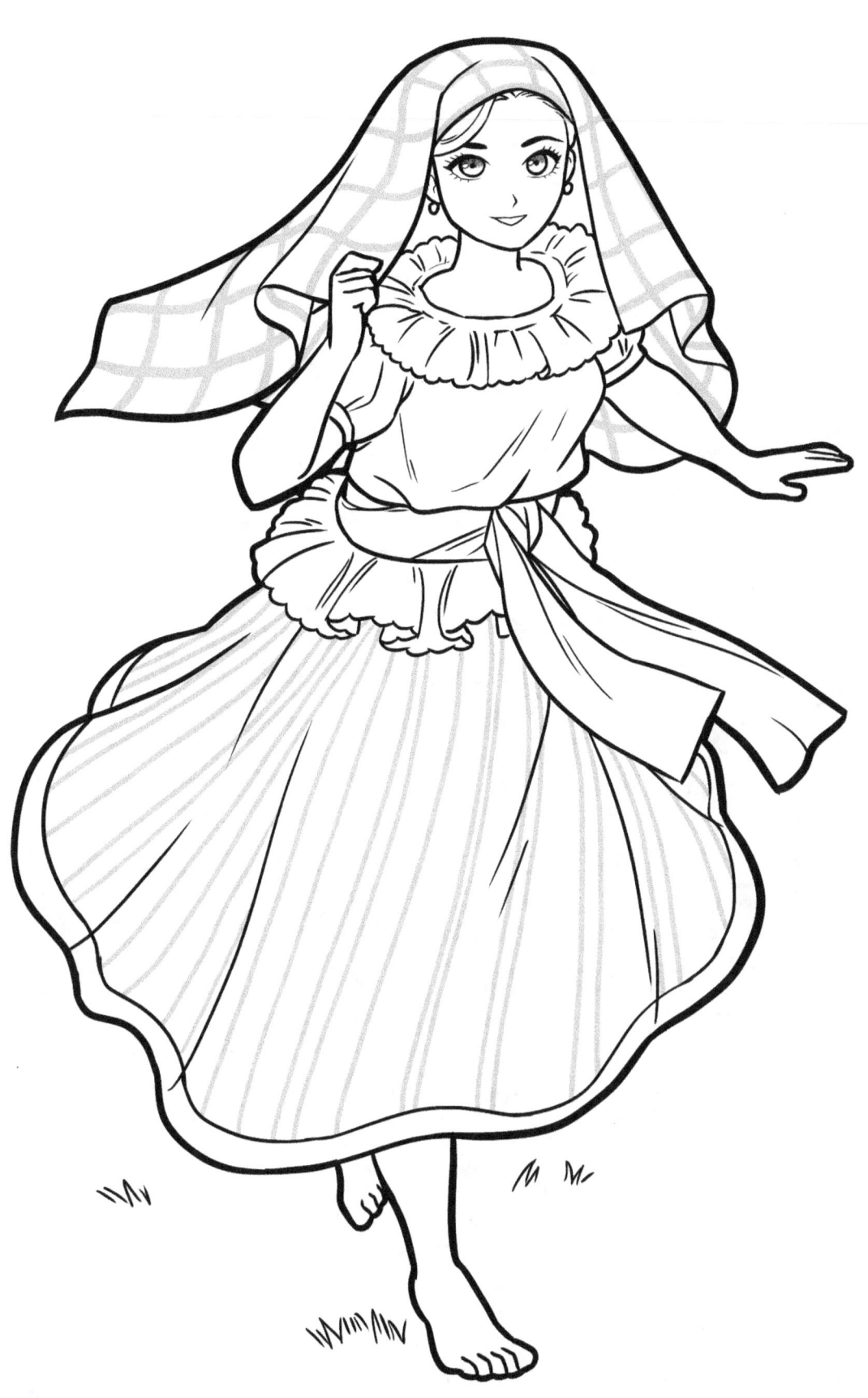

Tlaxcala

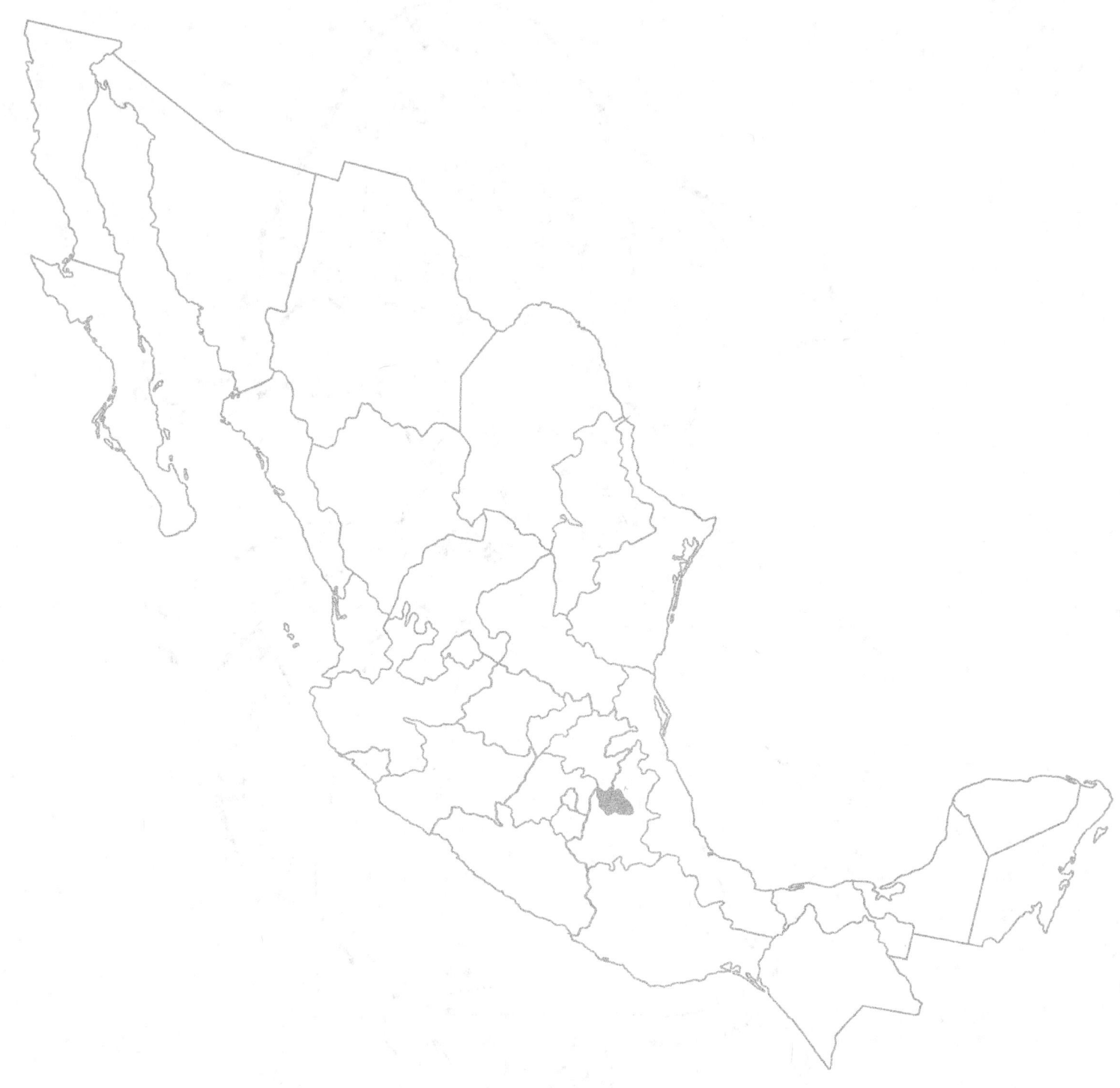

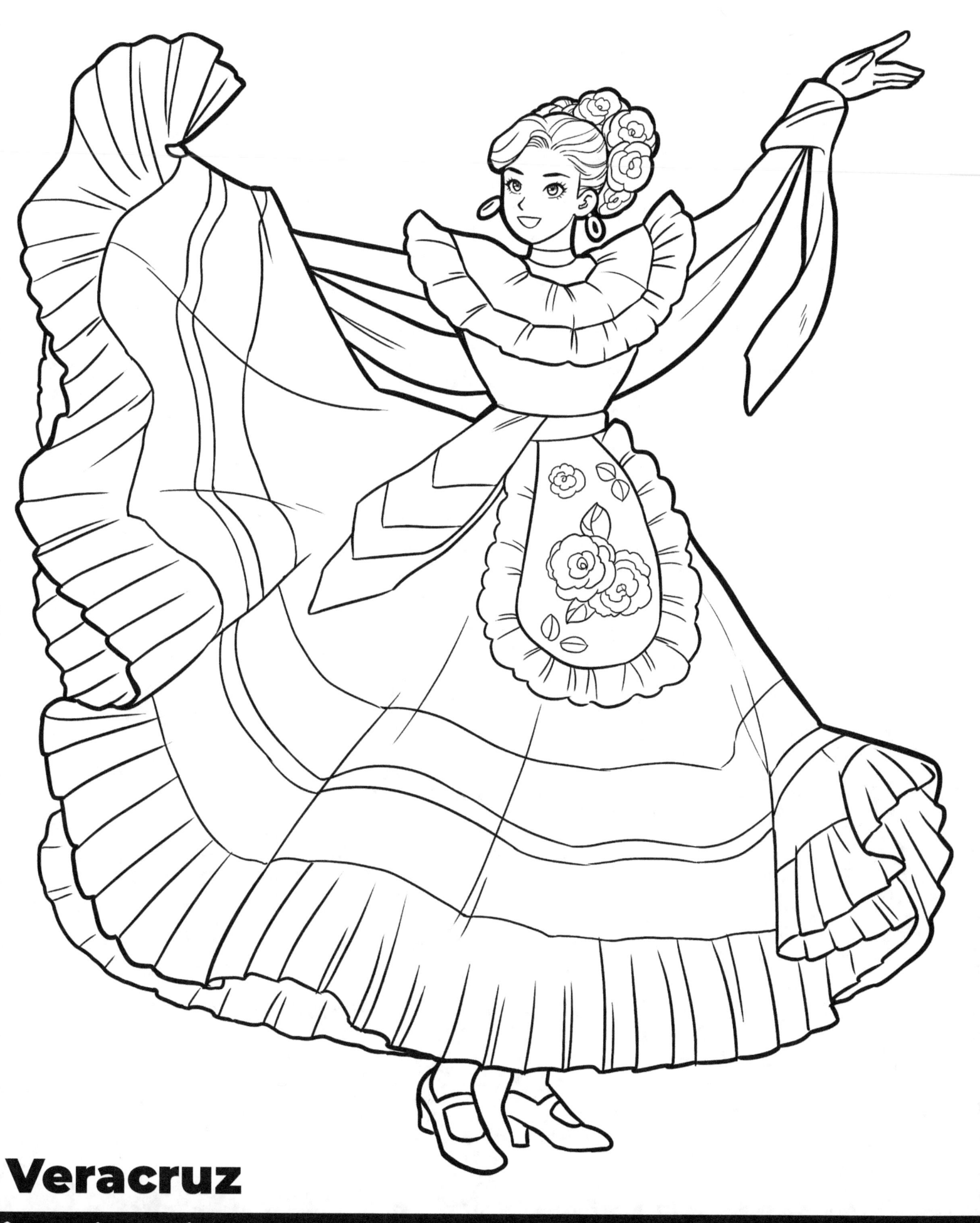

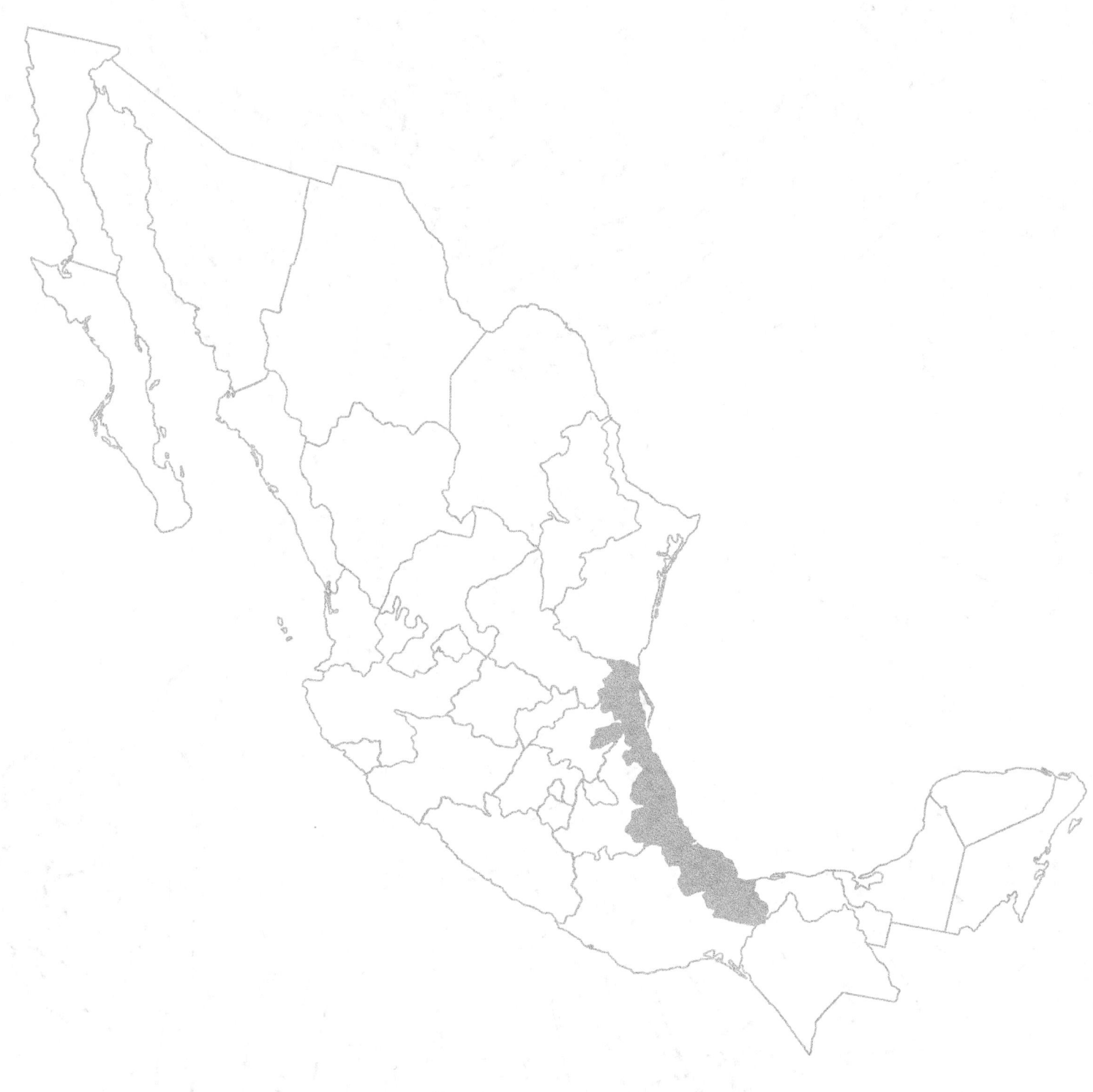

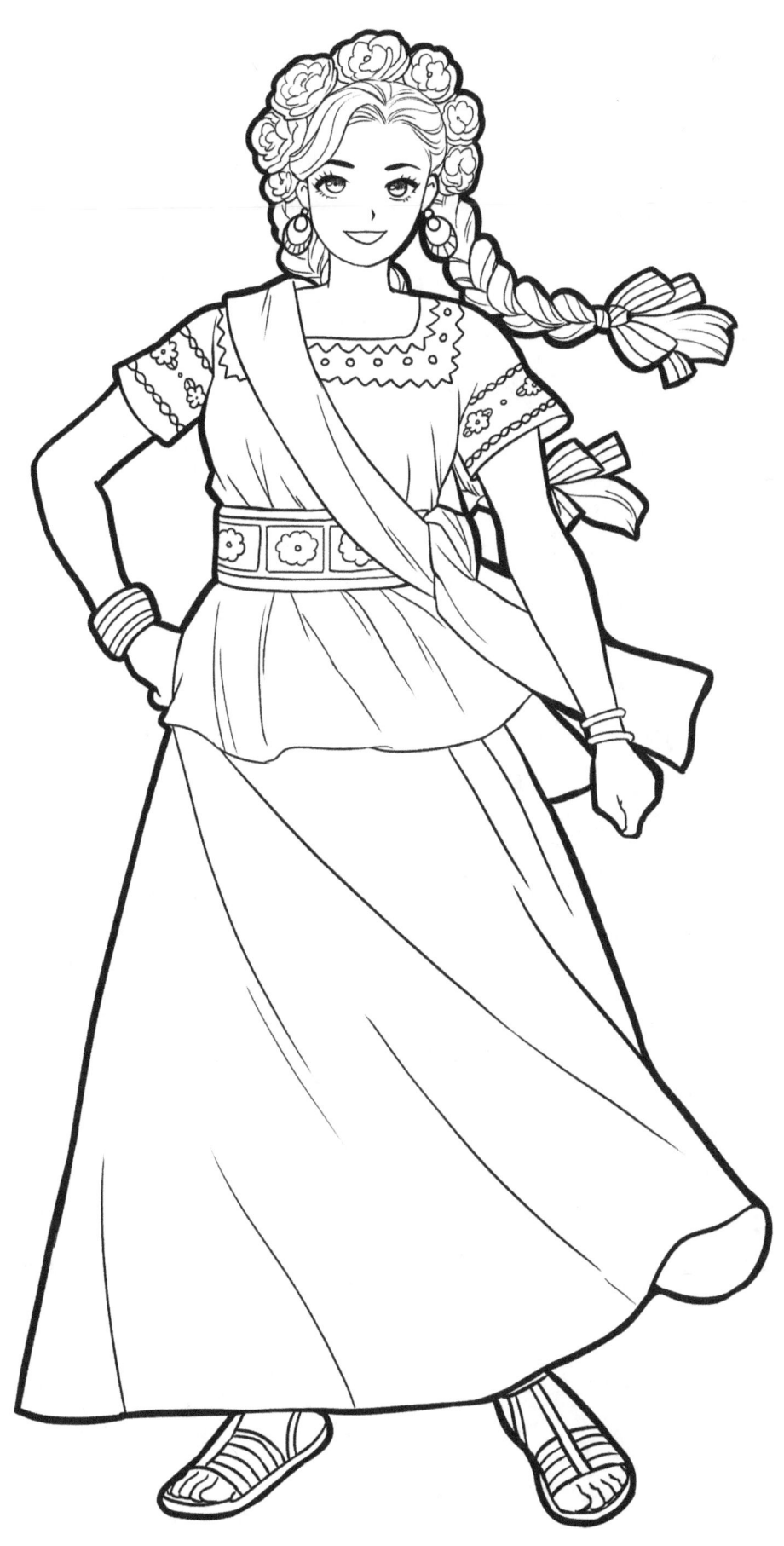

Xochimilco

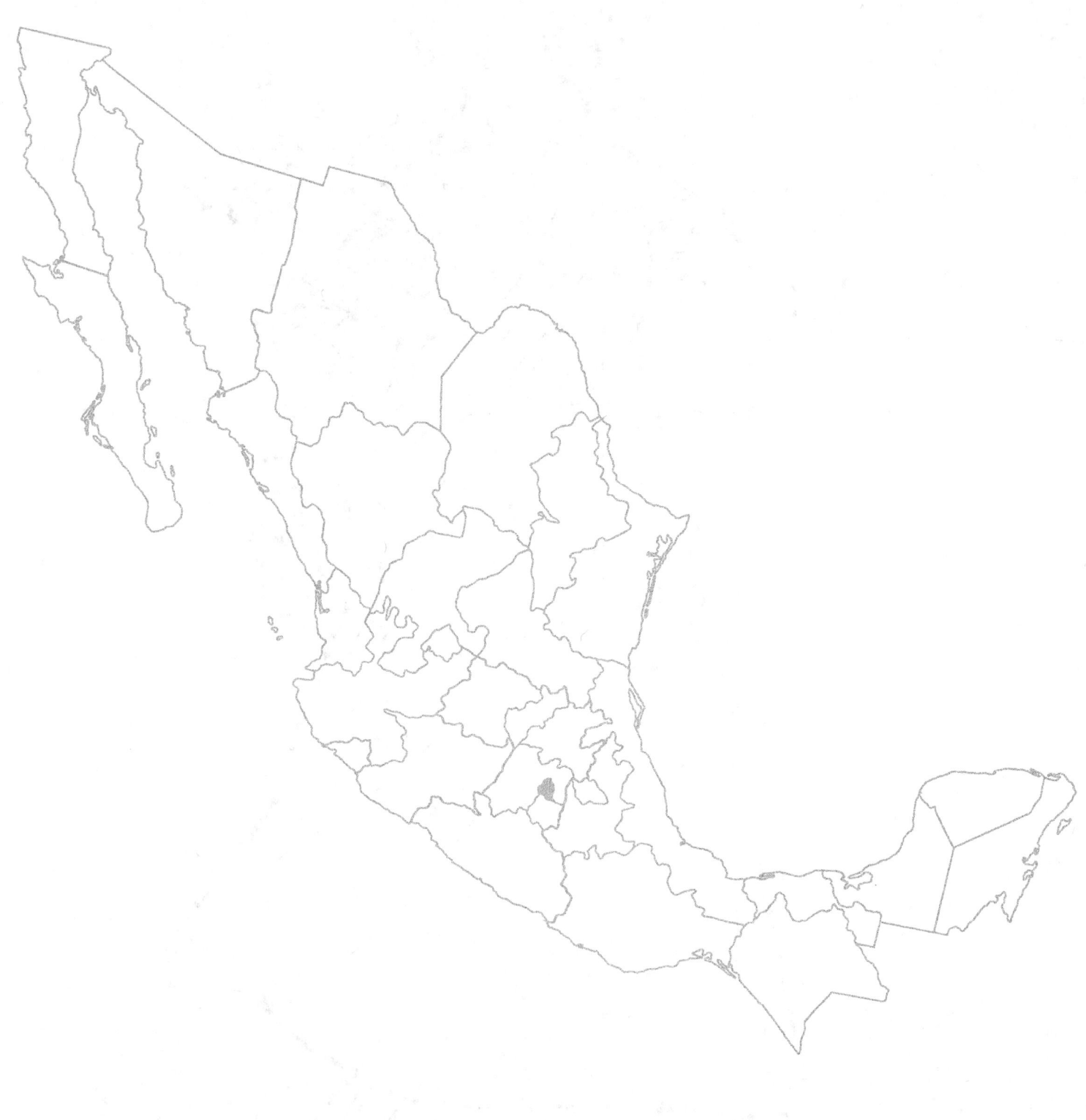

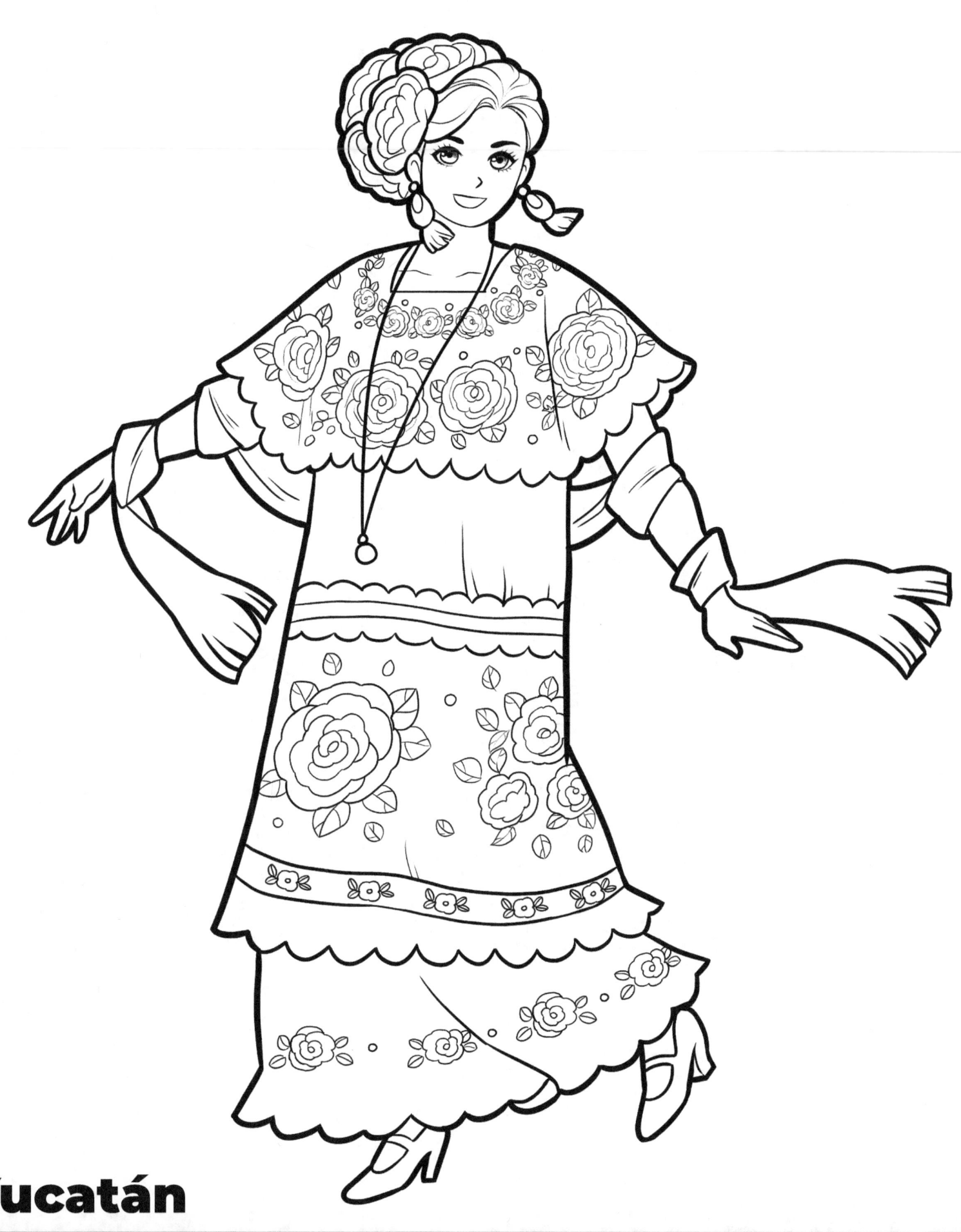
Yucatán

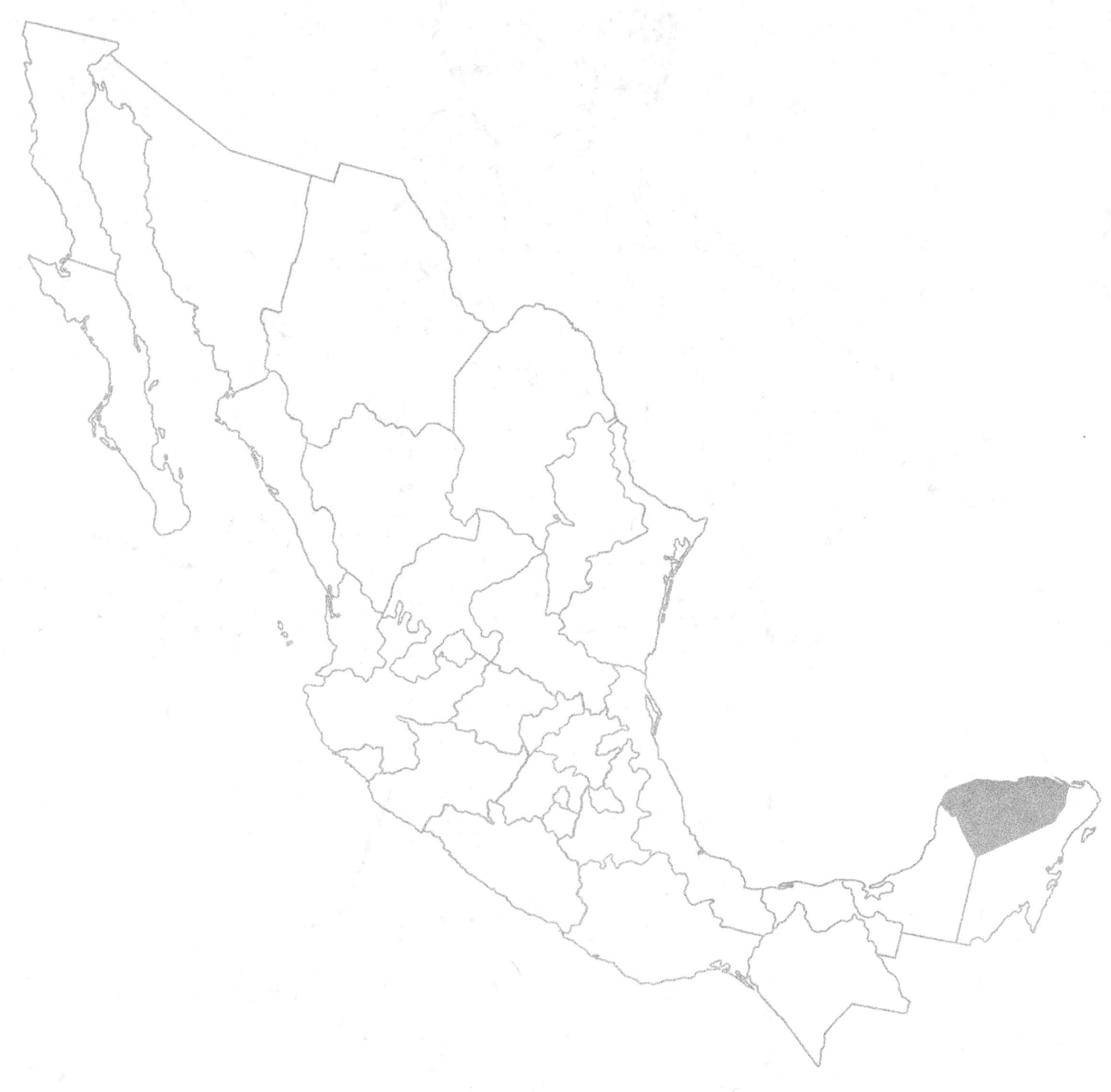

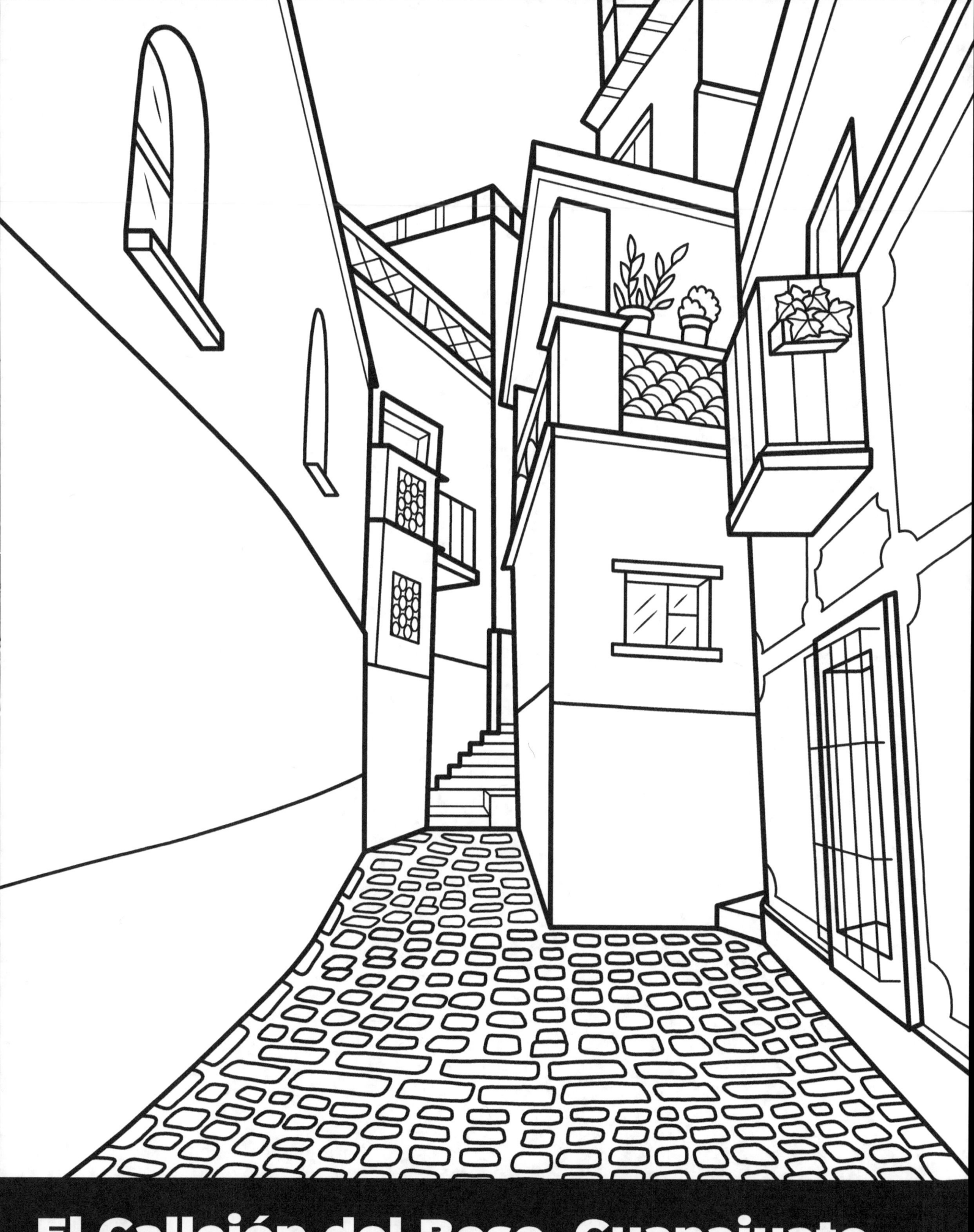
El Callejón del Beso, Guanajuato

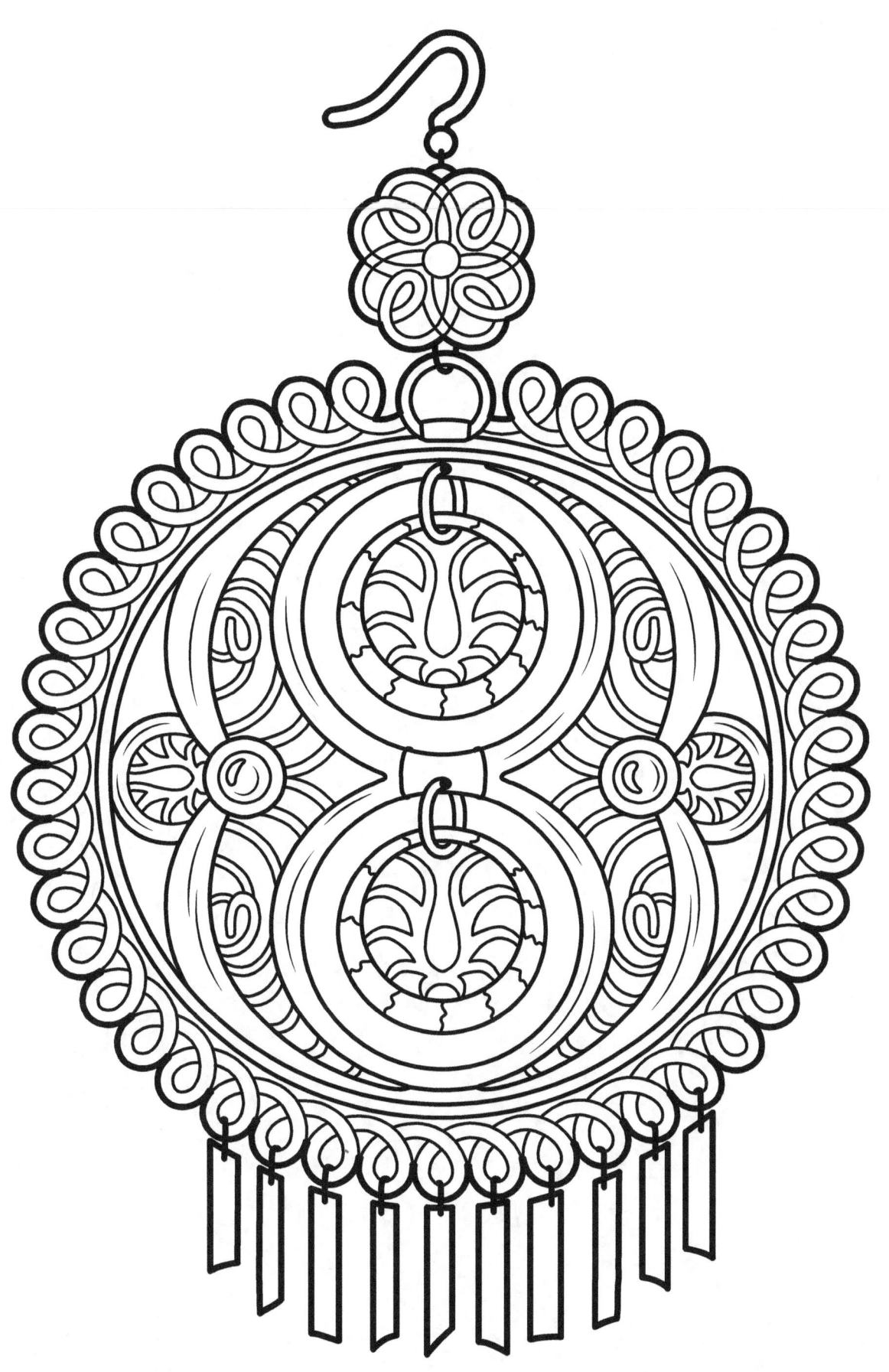

Arete

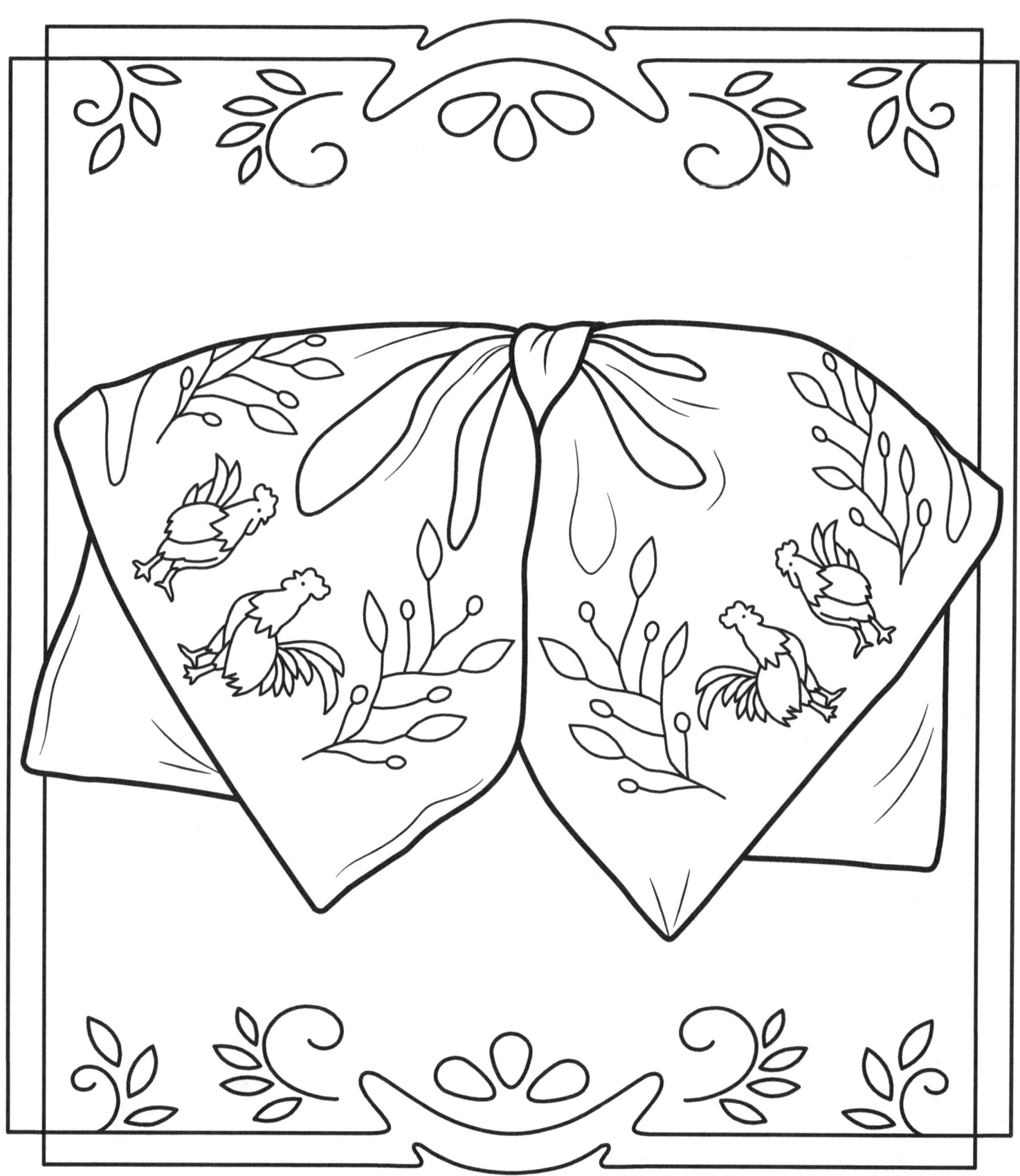

Corbata de Charro

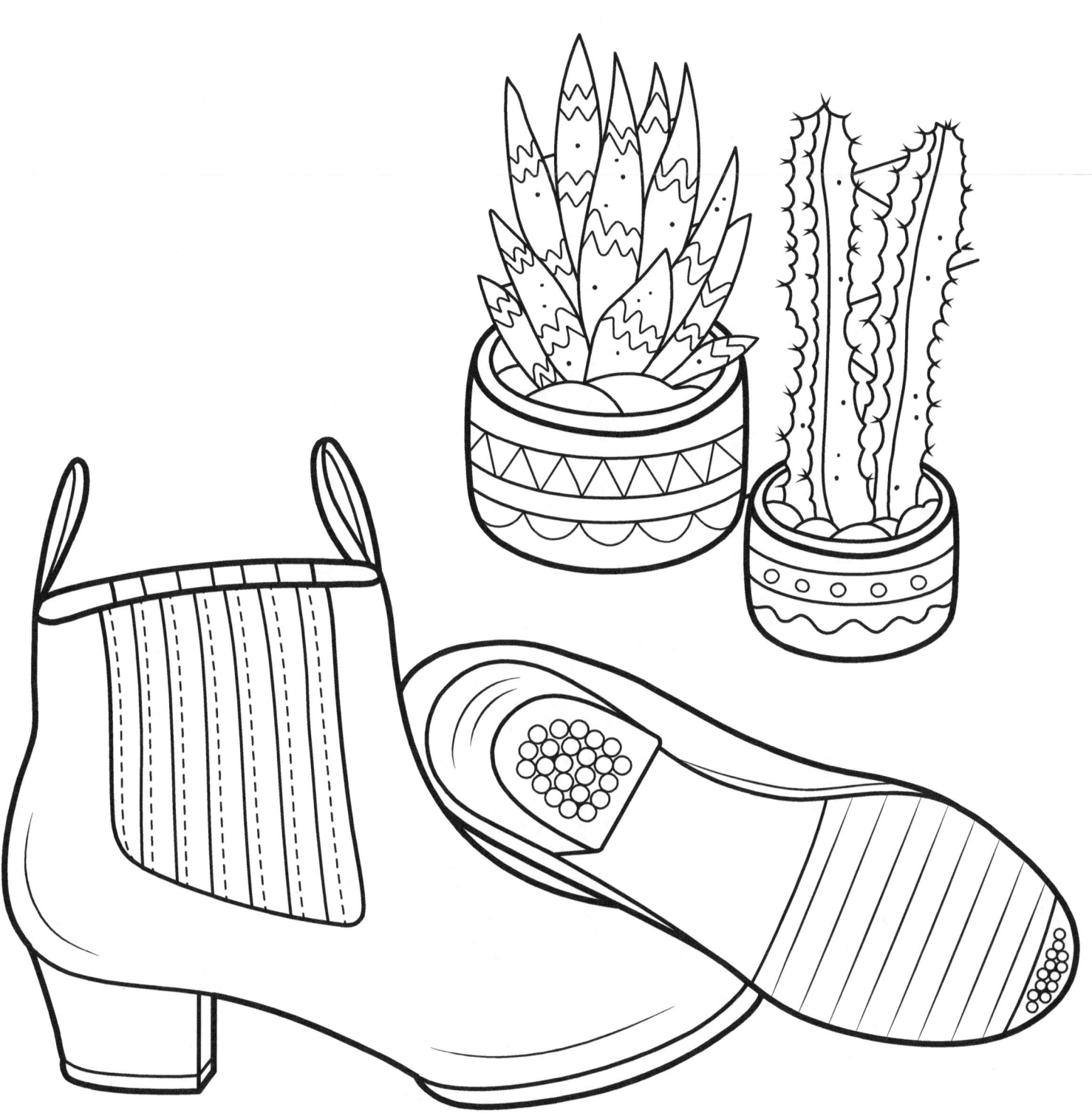

Botines de Charro

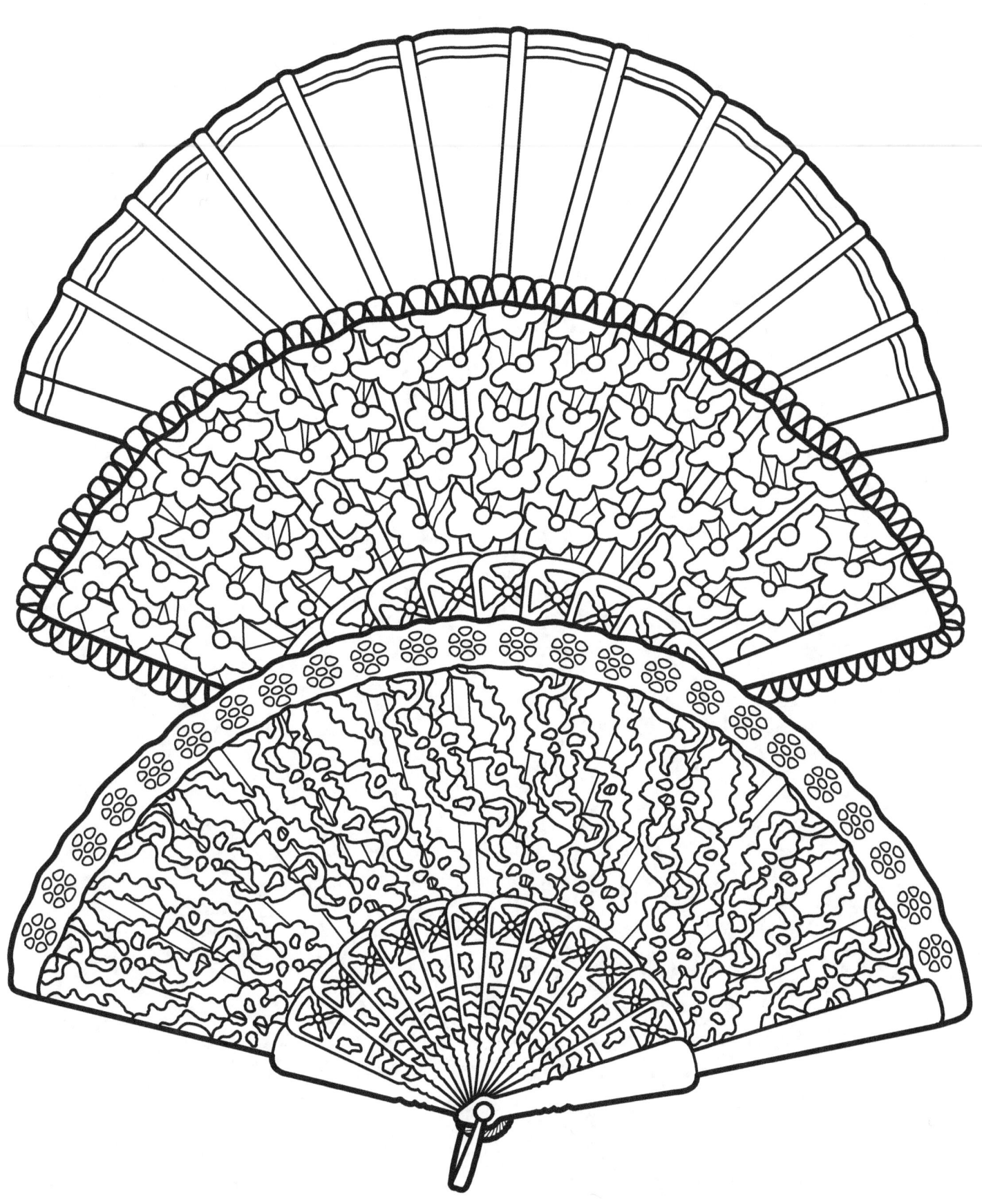

Abanico

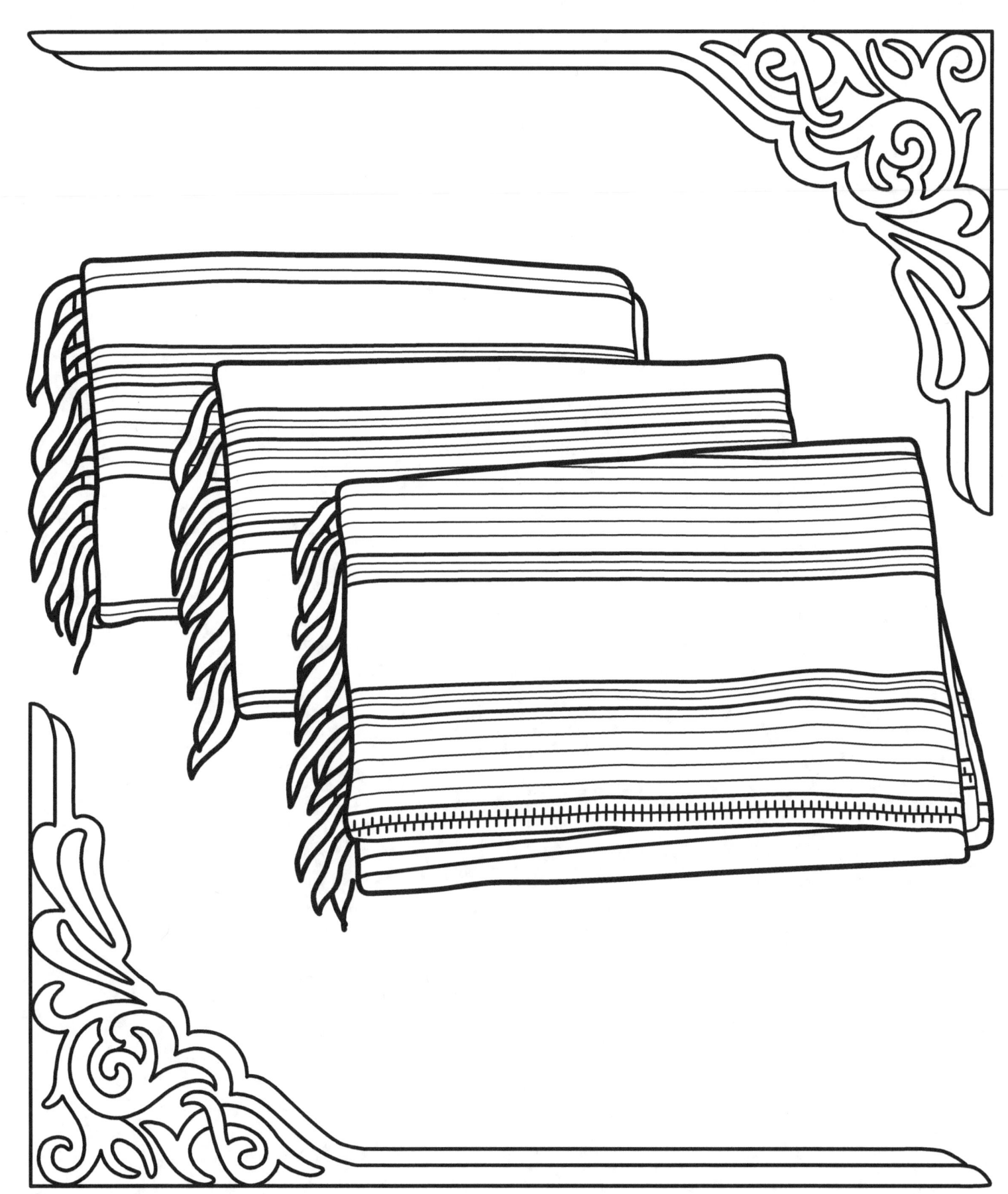

Zarape

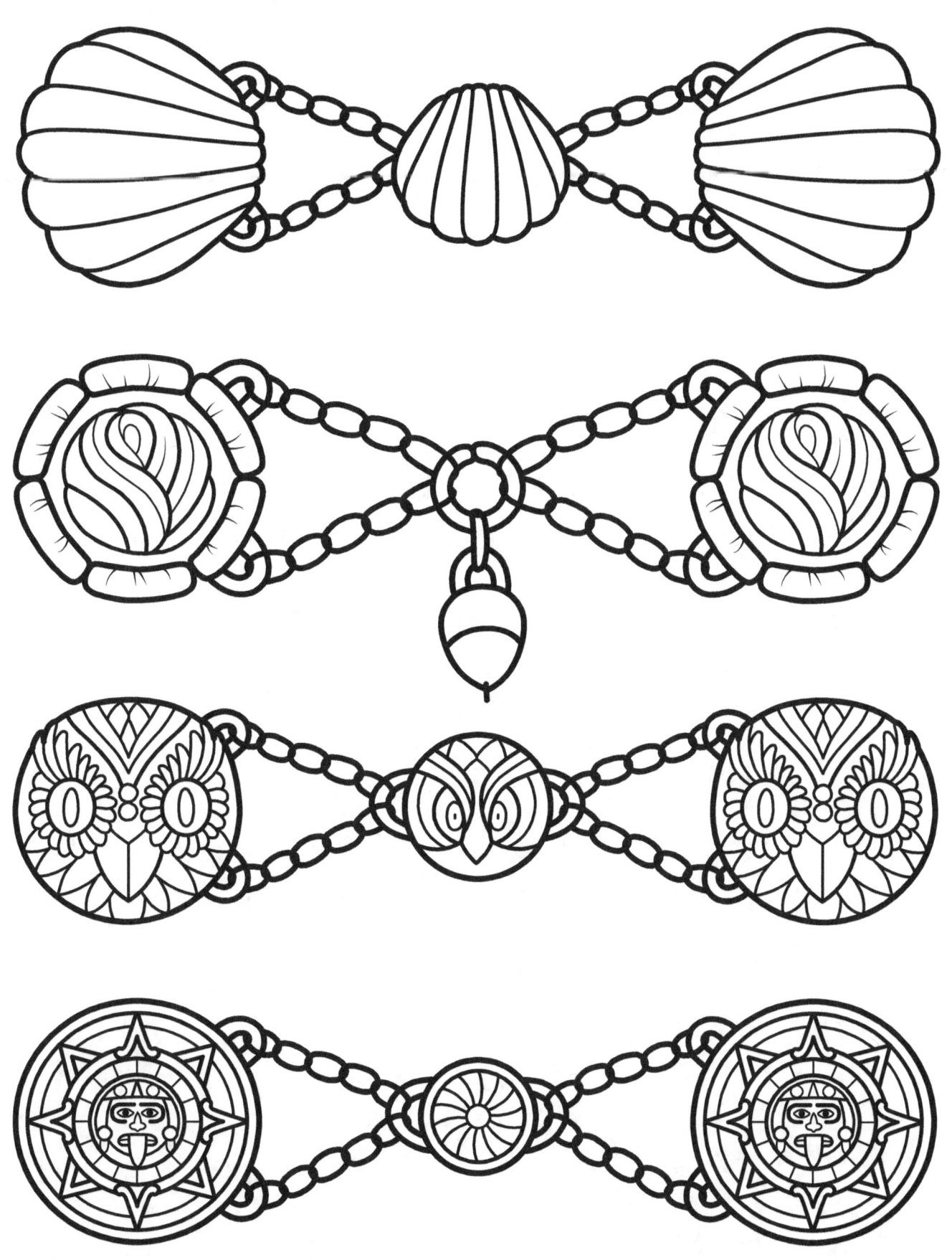

Botonadura

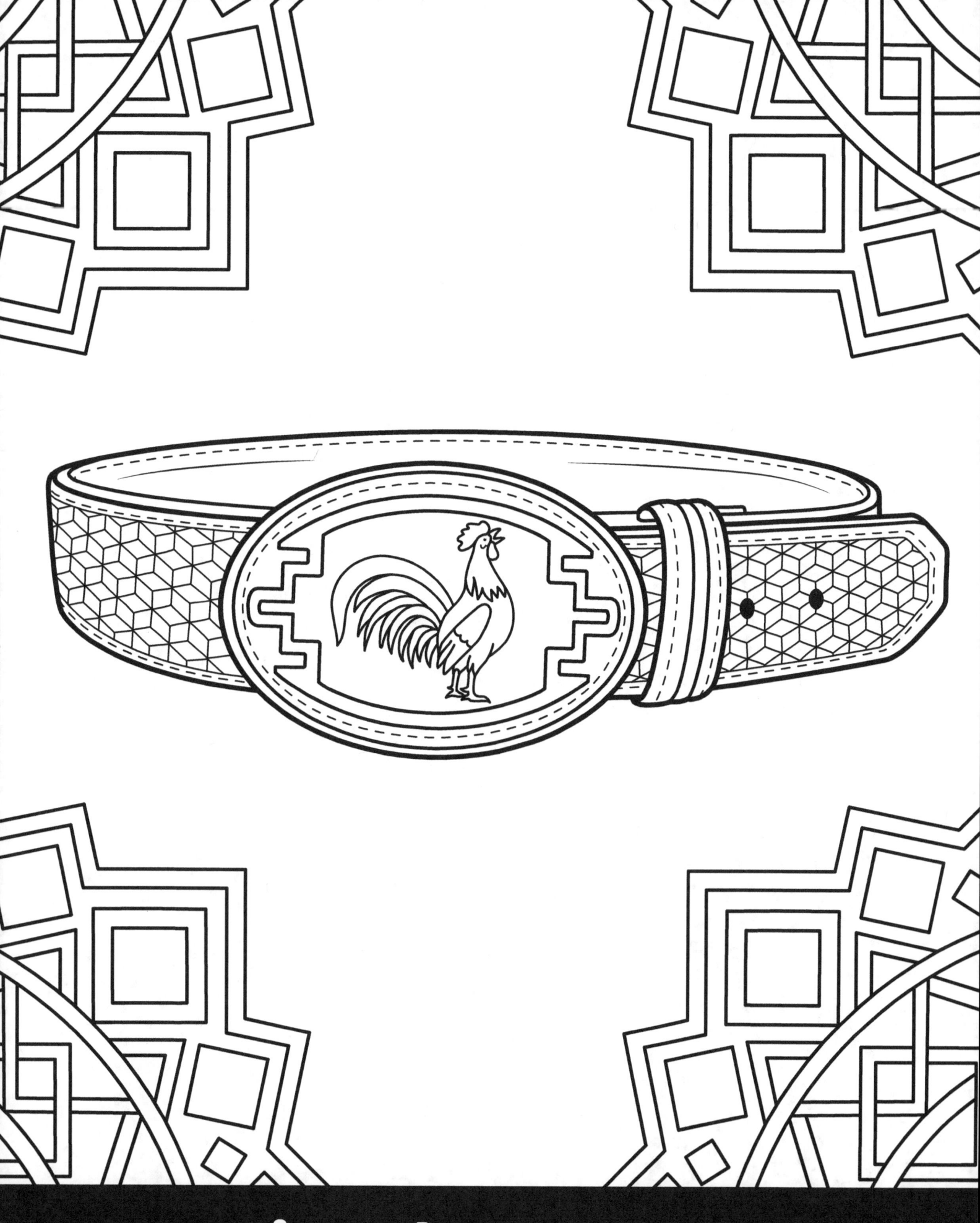

Cinturón de Charro

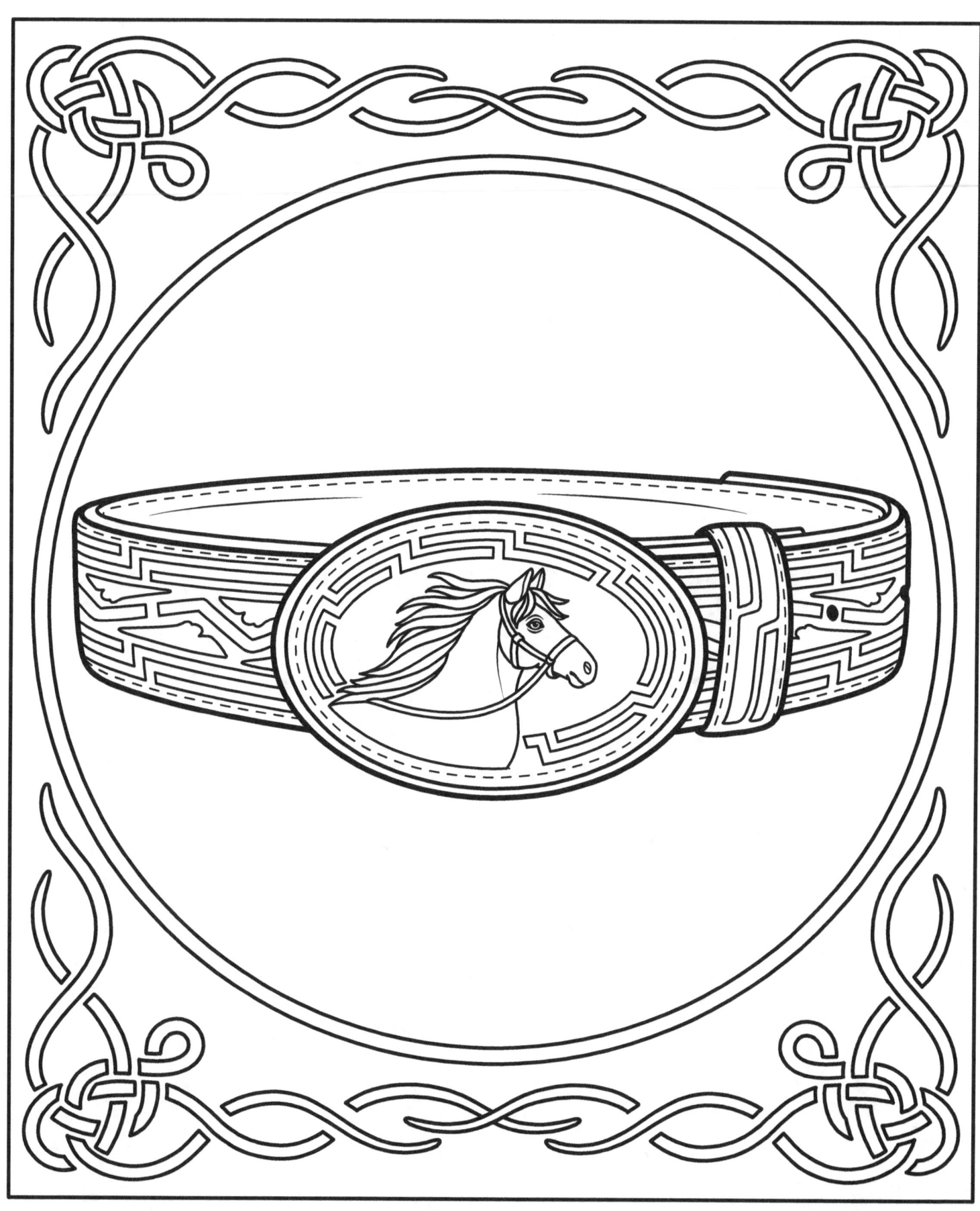

Cinturón de Charro

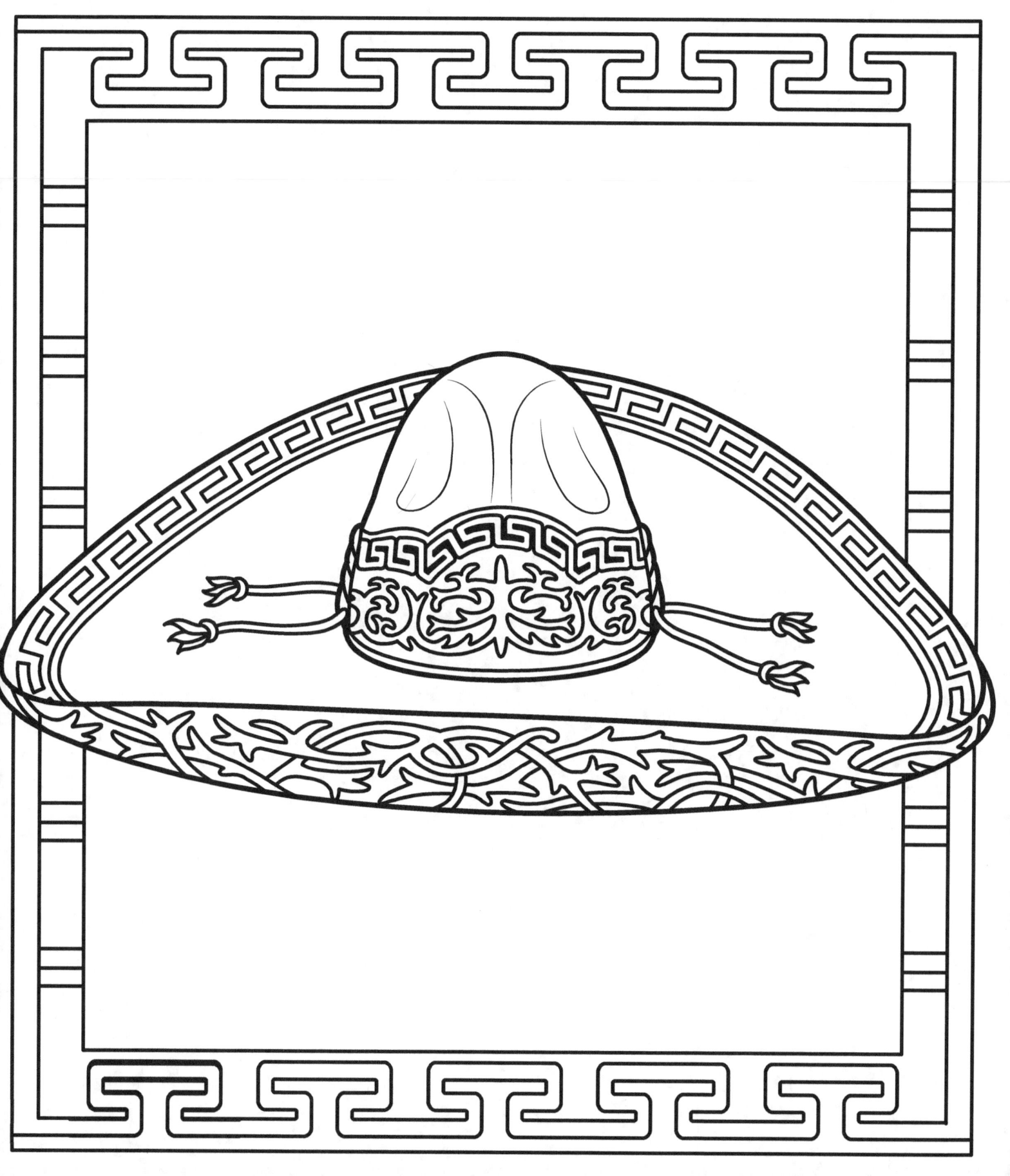

Sombrero de Charro

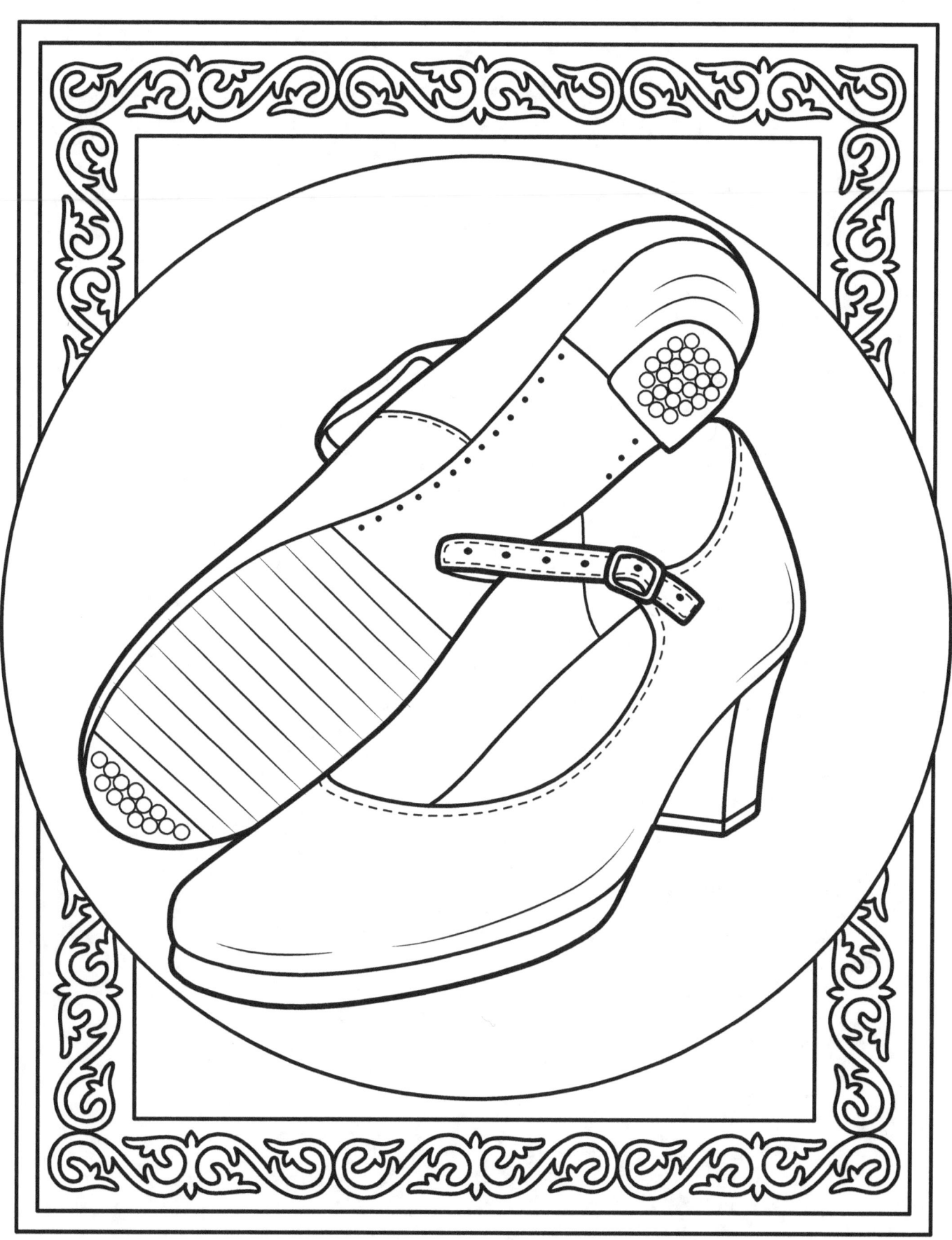

Zapatillas Folkloricas

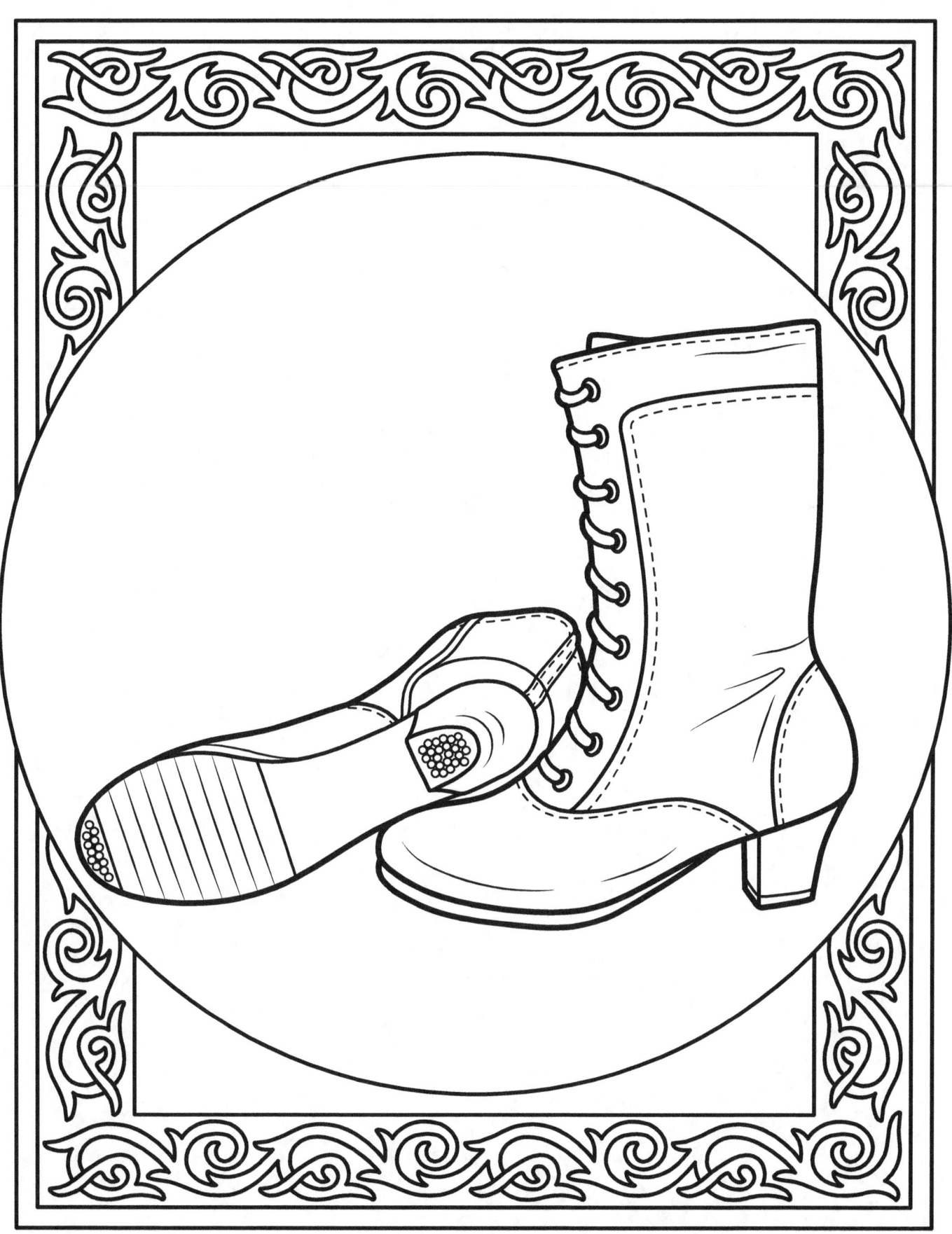

Botas Folkloricas

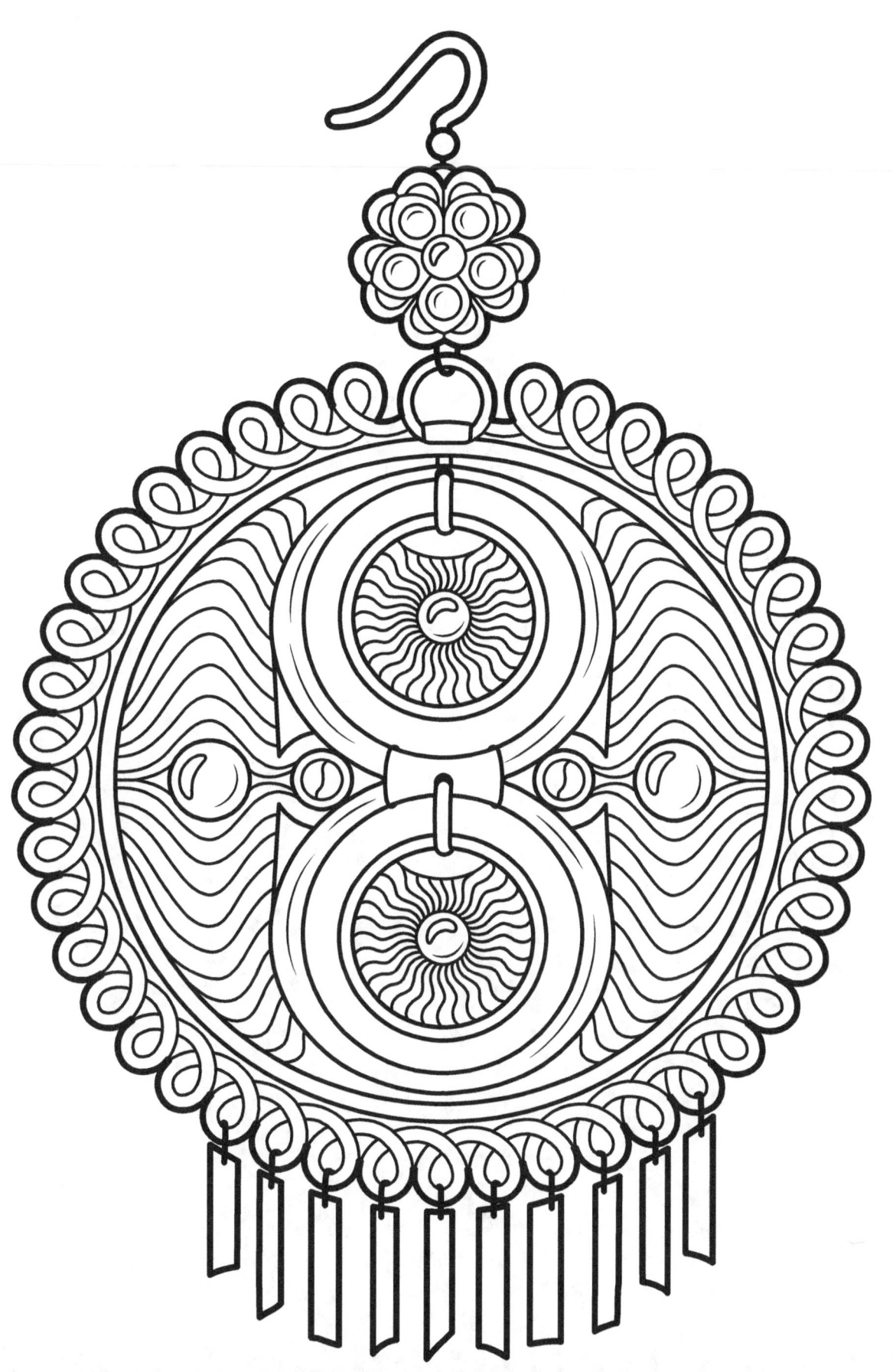

Arete

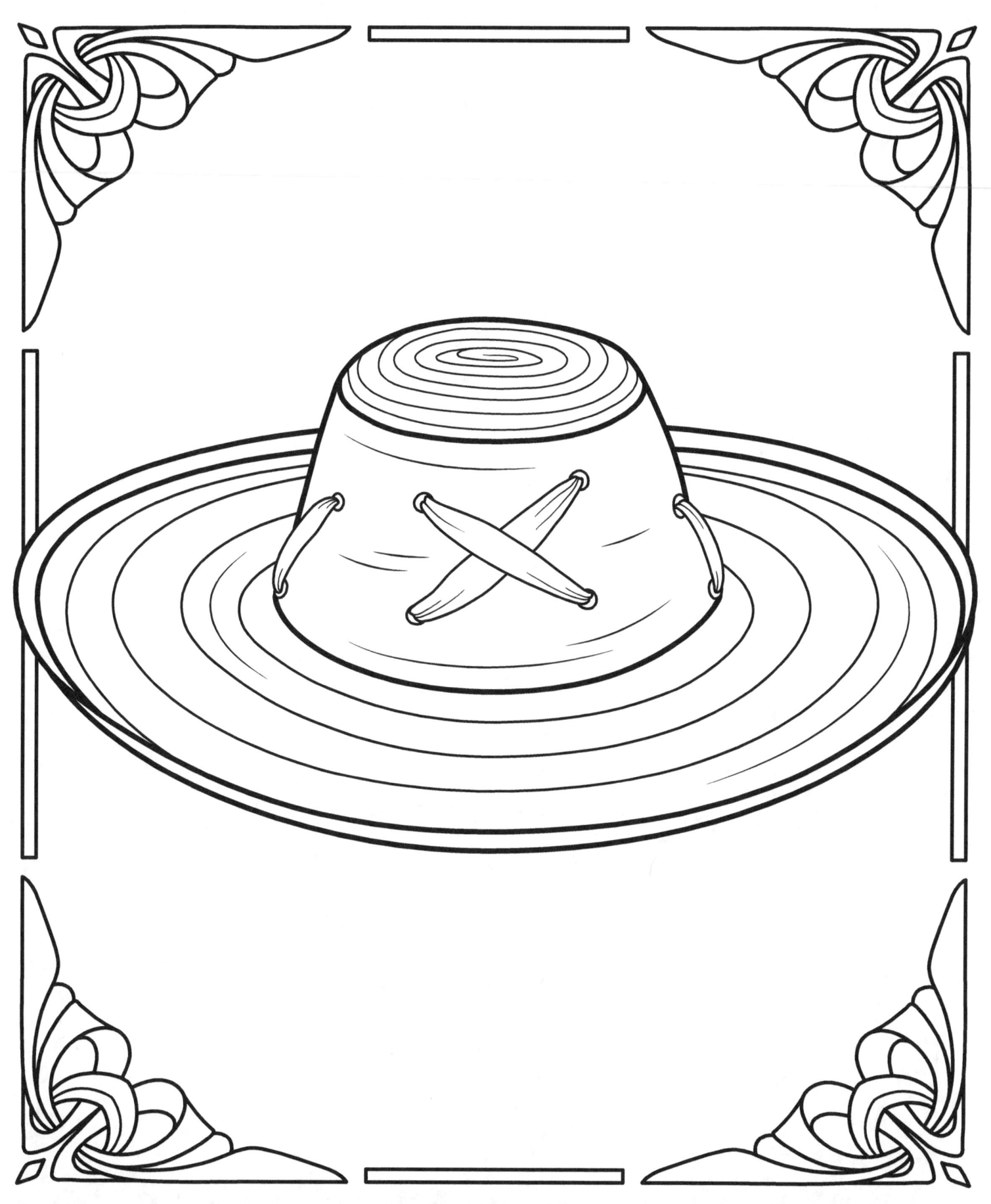

Sombrero de Michoacán

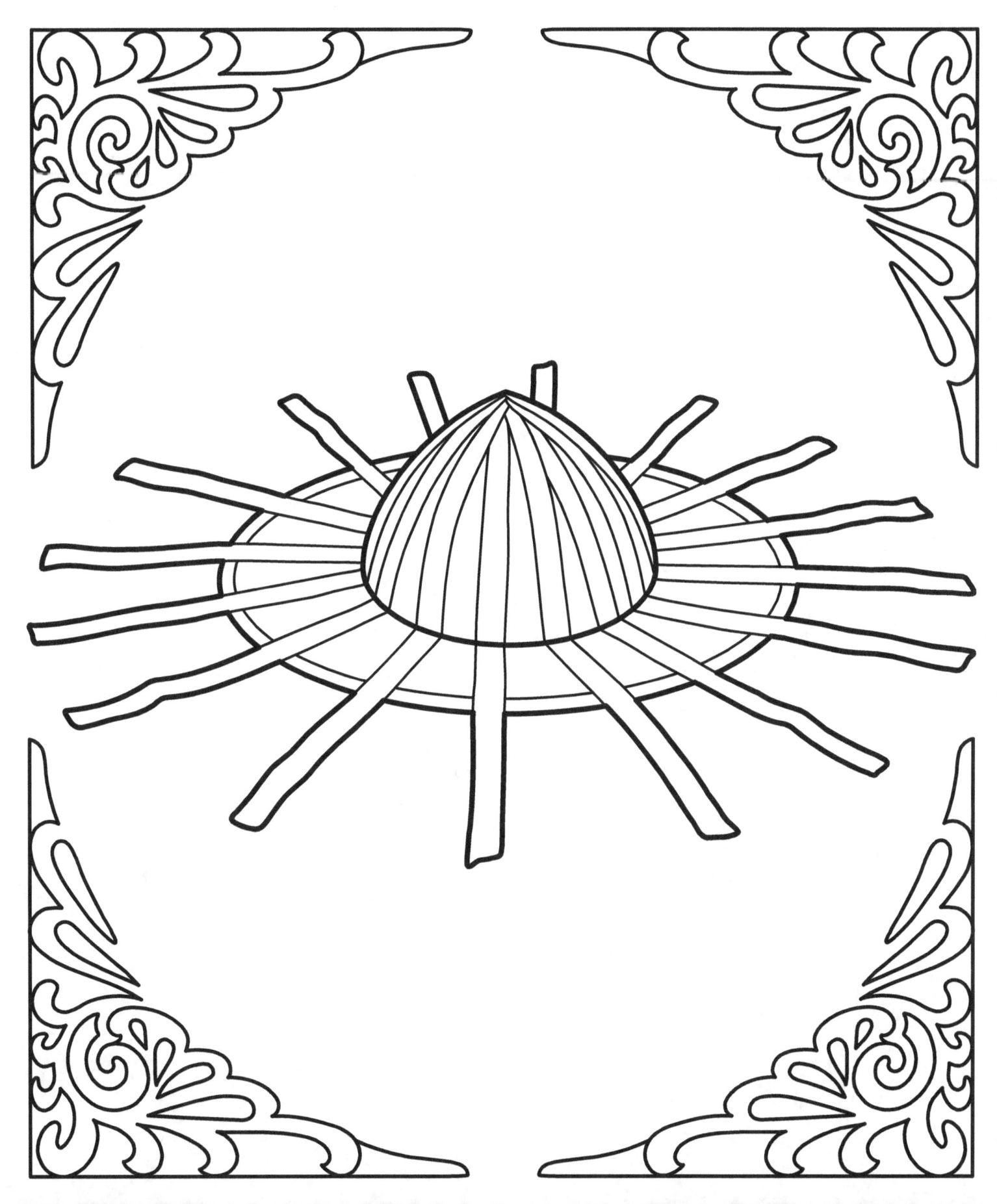

Sombrero de Paja - Viejitos

Peineta

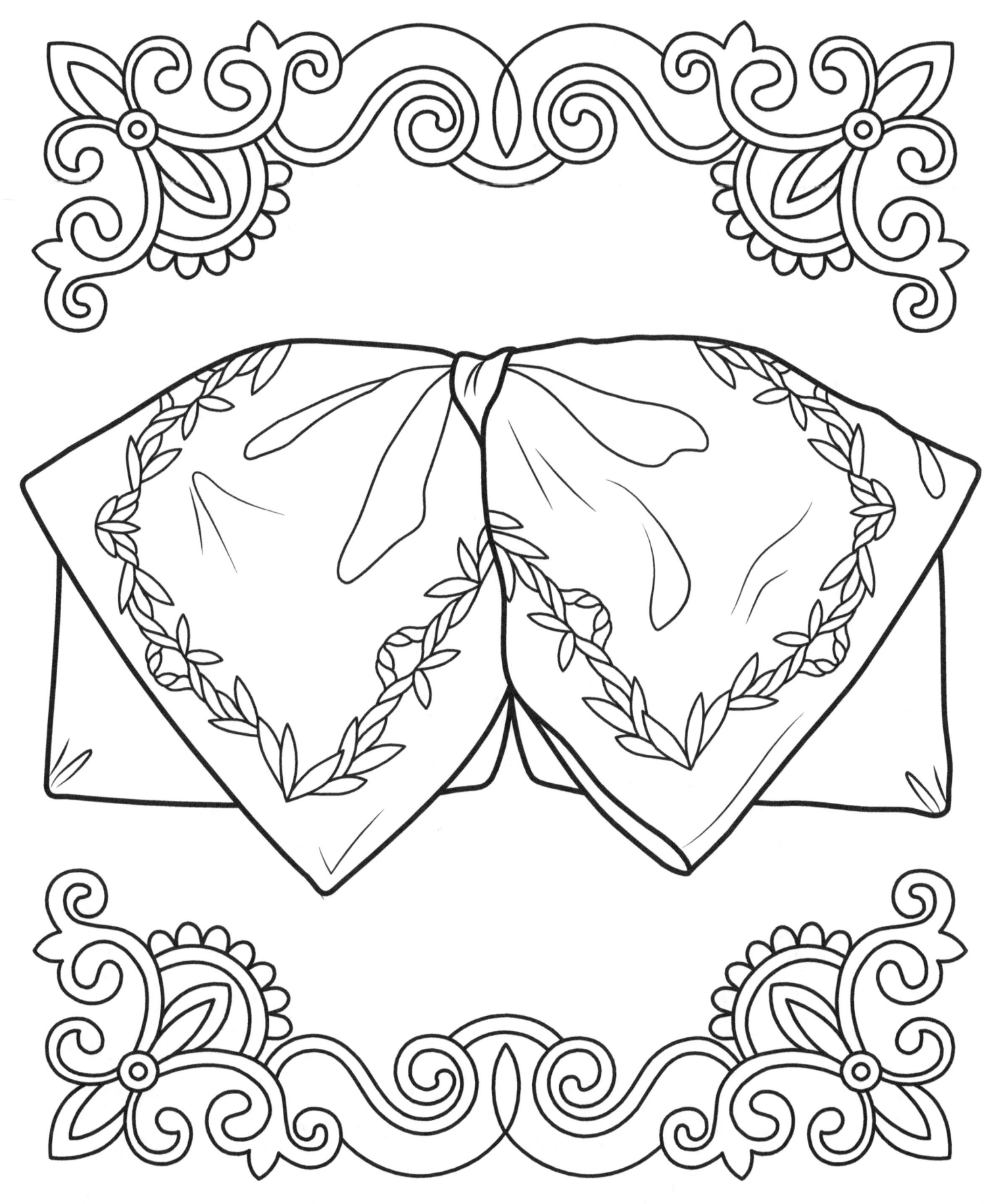
Corbata de Charro

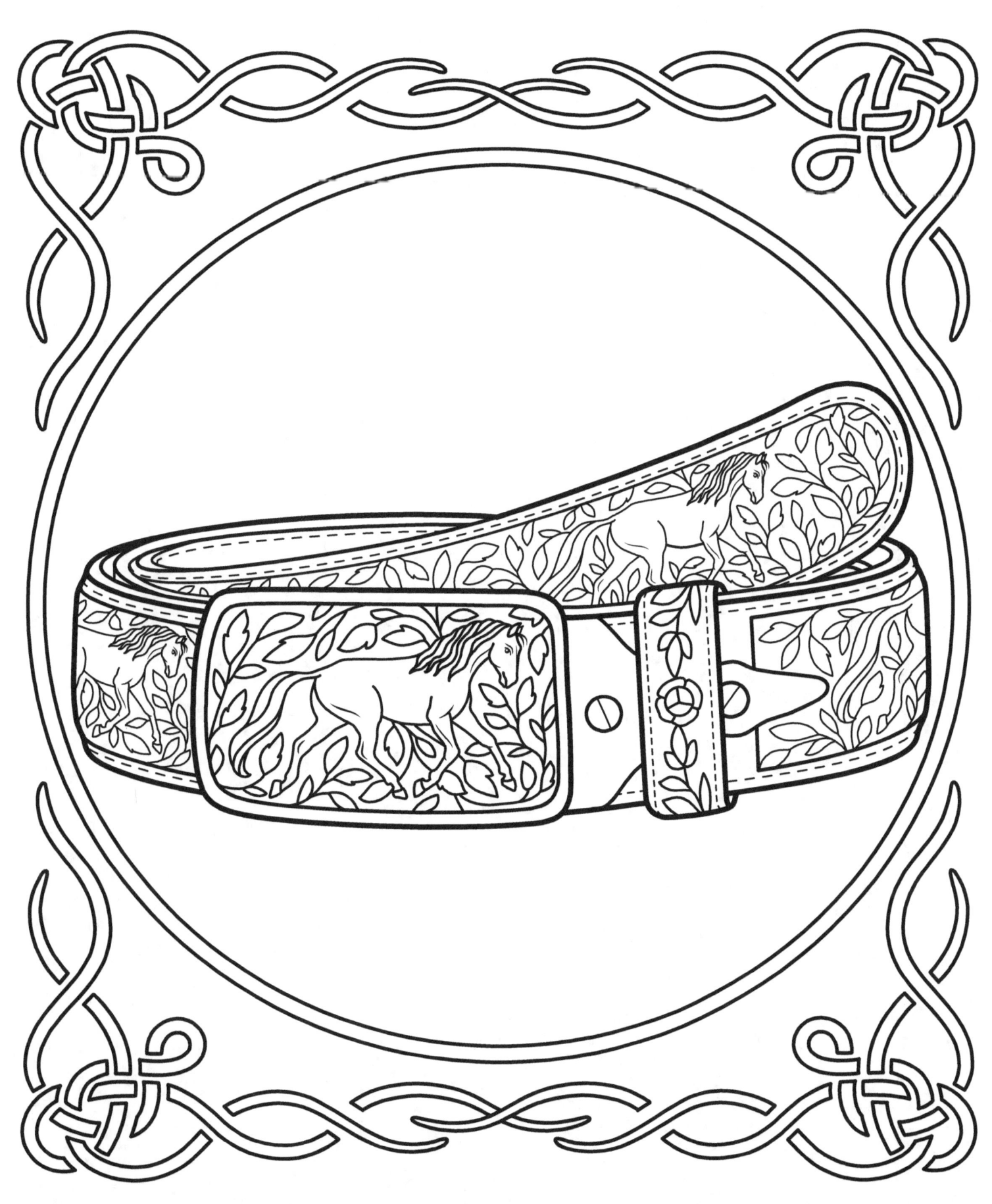

Cinturón de Charro

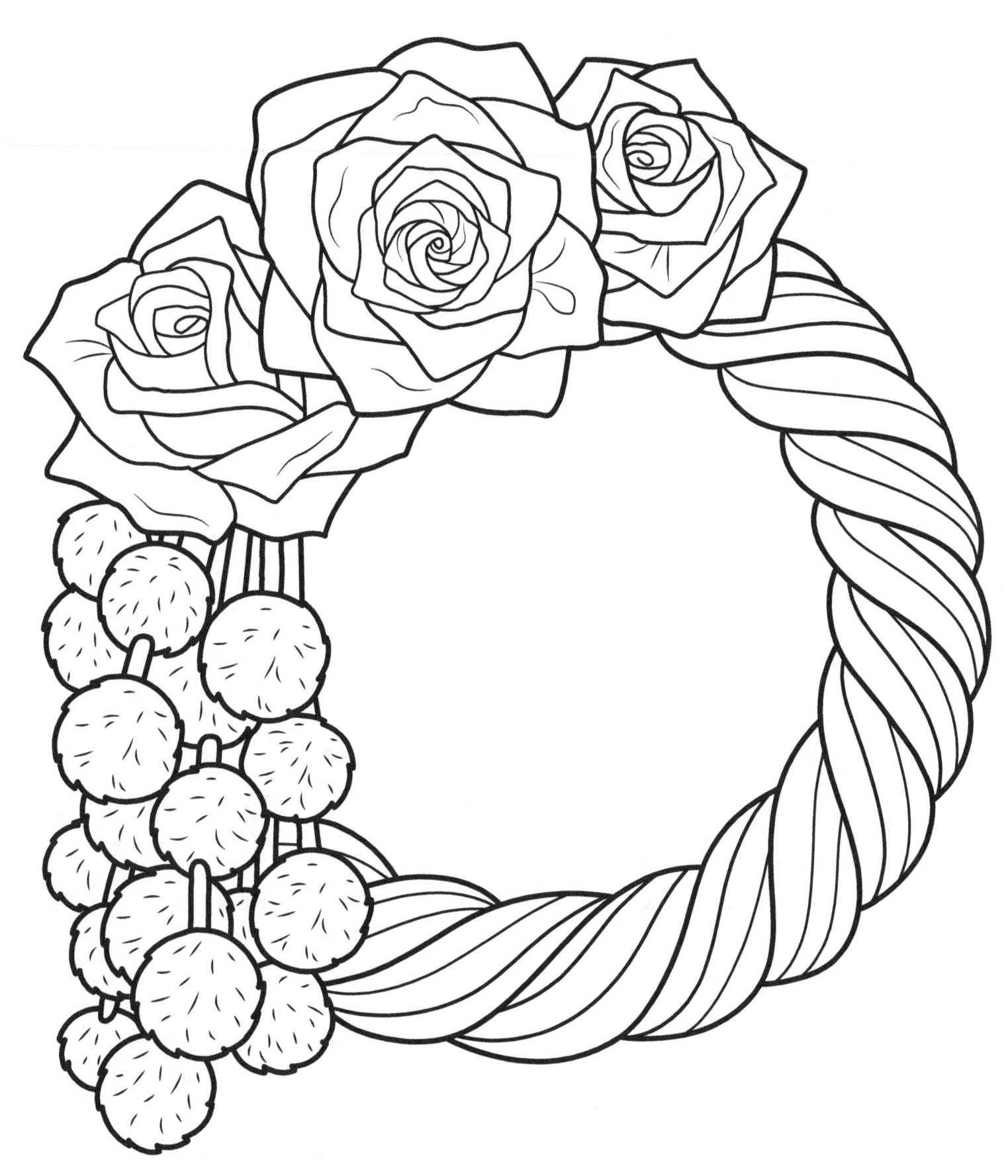

Tocado de Guerrero

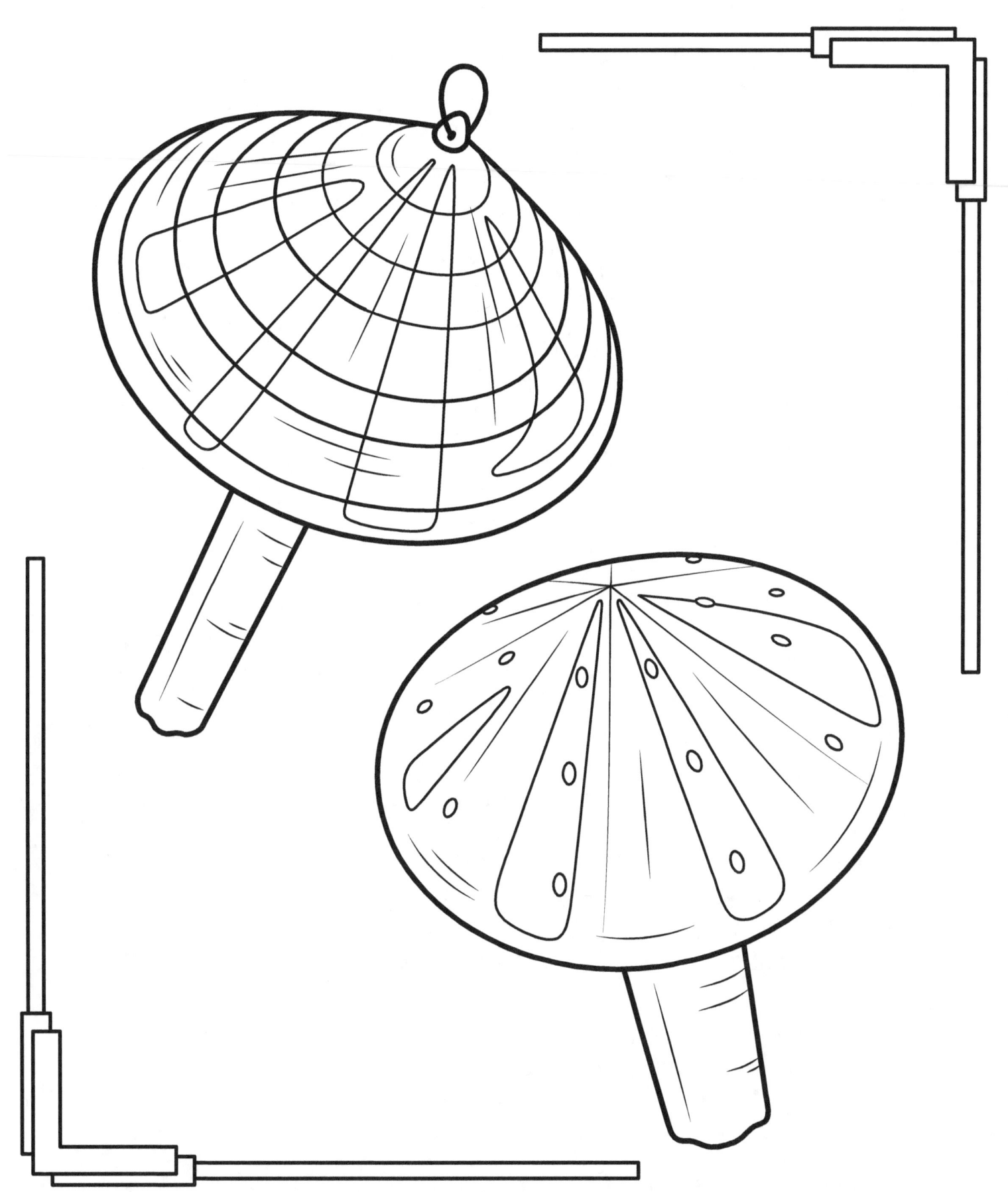

Sonaja

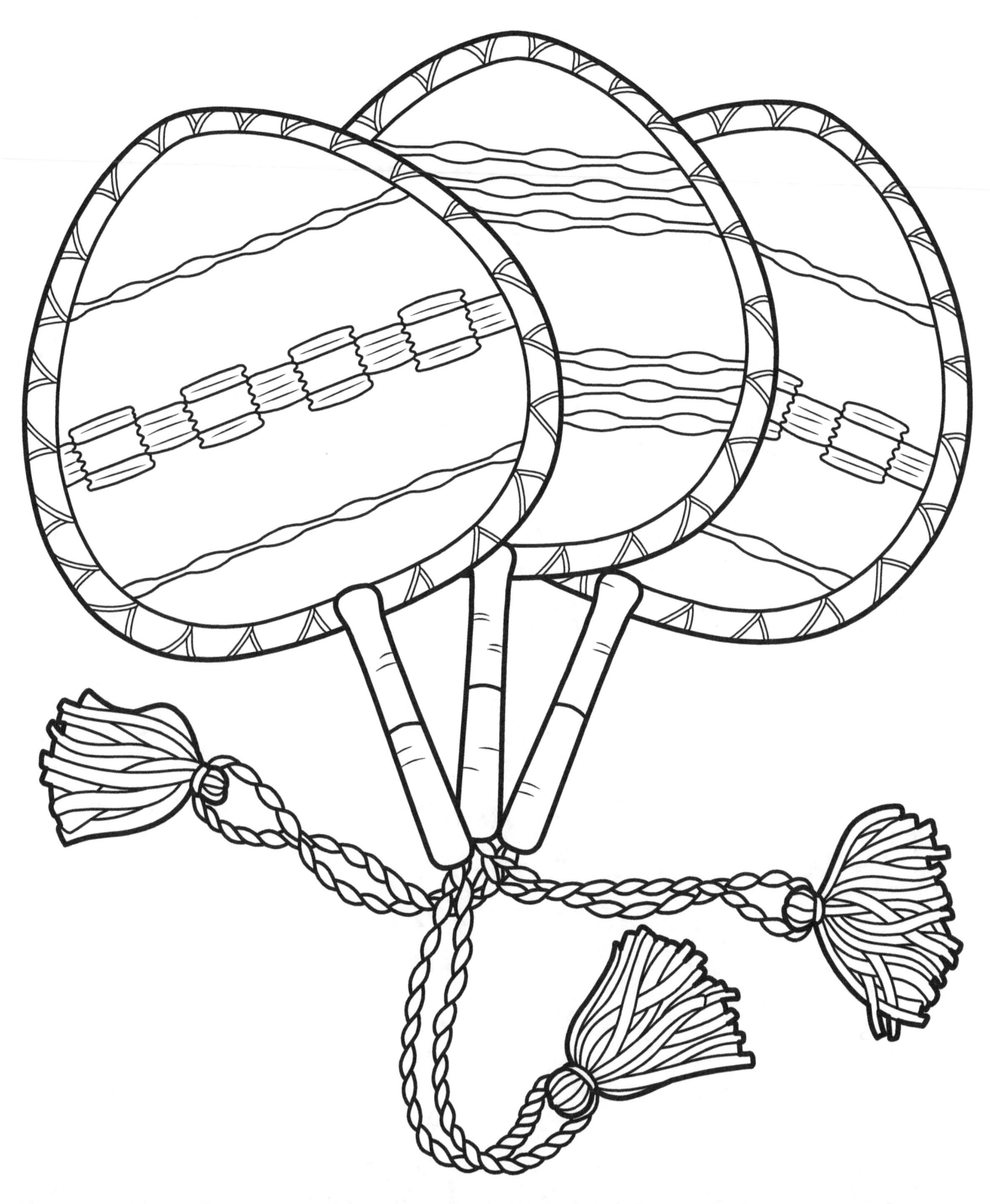

Abanicos de Palma

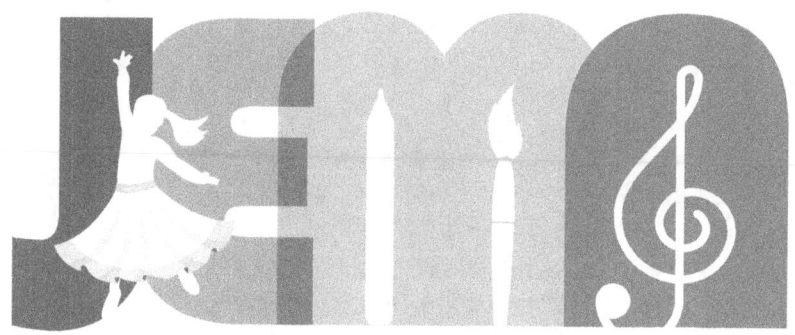

ABOUT US
Juventud Enriquecimiento Musica y Artes Foundation (JEMA)

MISSION
To enrich our youth through cultural music and arts.

VISION STATEMENT
To foster the enrichment of youth by encouraging awareness and appreciation of cultural music, visual and performing arts, education, literacy, and support community events and programs for youth.

Folklórico is a unique art that has been pivotal in enriching the public as well as the artists with knowledge about the culture of various states and regions within Mexico. With time, artists become knowledgeable at identifying music, lyrics, choreography, and costumes with their birth regions.

SOBRE NOSOTROS
Fundación Juventud Enriquecimiento Música y Artes

LA MISIÓN
Enriquecer a nuestra juventud con música y artes culturales.

LA VISIÓN
Promover el enriquecimiento de la juventud fomentando el conocimiento y el aprecio por la música cultural, las artes visuales y escénicas, la educación, la alfabetización y el apoyo de eventos y programas comunitarios para jóvenes.

El folklórico es un arte único que ha sido fundamental para enriquecer al público y a los artistas con conocimientos sobre la cultura de varios estados y regiones de México. Con el tiempo, los artistas se familiarizan y se identifican con la la música, la letra, la coreografía y el vestuario de sus regiones de natales.

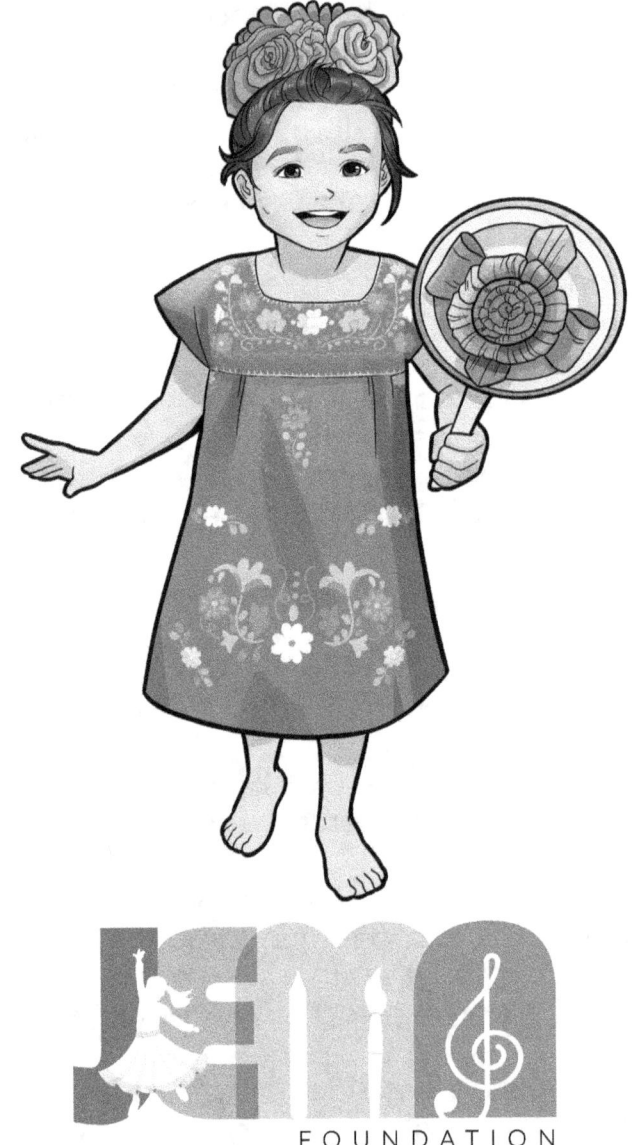

Printed in the U.S.A.

Juventud Enriquecimiento Musica y Artes Foundation
Post Office Box 845, Visalia, California 93279
jemafoundation.org | info@jemafoundation.org

www.ingramcontent.com/pod-product-compliance
Lightning Source LLC
Chambersburg PA
CBHW081436220526
45466CB00008B/2405